THE SPIRIT OF GOD

by Thomas Hopko

MOREHOUSE-BARLOW CO. INC.
WILTON, CONN.

INTRODUCTION

We likewise believe in the Holy Spirit,
The Lord and Giver of Life,
Who proceeds from the Father,
And abides in the Son;

Who is adored and glorified
With the Father and the Son
As co-essential and co-eternal with Them;

Who is the true and authoritative Spirit of God,
The Source of wisdom and life and sanctification;

Who is God together with the Father and the Son,
And is thus proclaimed;
Who is uncreated, full, creative, almighty;
Who is ever-active, all powerful, infinite in strength;

Who rules over all creation, but is not ruled,
Who deifies everything, but is not deified,
Who fills all things, but is not filled,
Who is participated, but does not participate,
Who sanctifies, but is not sanctified,
Who receives the intercessions of all, and is The Intercessor; ·

Who is like the Father and the Son in all things;
Who proceeds from the Father,
And is communicated through the Son,
And is participated in by all creation;

Who through Himself creates and gives being to all things,
And sanctifies and preserves them;

Who is distinctly personal,
And exists in His own Person,
Indivisible and inseparable from the Father and the Son;

Who has all things that the Father and the Son have,
Except that He is not the Unbegotten Father,
Nor is He the Only-begotten Son.

St. John of Damascus
On the Orthodox Faith, Book I

i

Man is not genuinely human without the Spirit of God. This is the testimony of the Scripture and tradition of God's people. This is the witness of those made competent to disclose the meaning of things because of their living union with God. This is the doctrine of the prophets, apostles, and saints. This is the gospel of the Lord Jesus Christ.

Man is truly man, God's created image and likeness, when he lives by the Spirit of his Lord. The Holy Spirit liberates man from captivity to dust and makes man conscious of his divine and everlasting destiny. The Holy Spirit renders man free from all that blinds and binds him and makes him a fool. Without the Spirit, man is captivated by the vain imaginations of the heart and mind, enslaved by the passions and lusts of the flesh, deadened and darkened by the powers of evil in the "elemental forces" of graceless existence.

St. Irenaeus in the second century said that man, by definition, is body, soul, and Holy Spirit: the creature formed to conform, through the Spirit, to the image of God who is the eternal Son and Word of God, the Lord Jesus Christ.

Everyone will allow that we are composed of a body taken from the earth, and a soul, which receives the Spirit from God.

For by the hands of the Father, that is, by the Son and the Spirit, man, and not merely a part of man, was made in the likeness of God. . . .for the perfect man consists in the commingling and the union of the soul receiving the Spirit of the Father, and the mixture of that fleshly nature which also was moulded after the image of God. . .the man becomes spiritual and perfect because of the outpouring of the Spirit, and this is he who was made in the image and likeness of God [which is Christ].

If in a man the Spirit is not united to the soul, this man is imperfect; he remains animal and carnal; he does have the image of God in his flesh, but he is not receiving the likeness through the Spirit. [Against Heresies]

This teaching is repeated in many ways by the holy people of God. St. Basil the Great (4th century) says man is the creature who, through the Holy Spirit, becomes divine by grace.

. . .so souls wherein the Spirit dwells, illumined by the Spirit, themselves become spiritual, and send forth their grace to others. Hence comes the knowledge of the future, the understanding of mysteries, the apprehension of what is hidden, the distribution of good gifts, the heavenly citizenship, a place in the choir of the angels,

joy without end, abiding in God, the being made like to God, and, highest of all, the being made god. [*On the Holy Spirit*]

St. Basil's brother, St. Gregory of Nyssa, says the same:

For this is the safest way to protect the good things you enjoy: by realizing how much your creator has honored you above all other creatures. He did not make the heavens in His image, nor the moon, the sun, the beauty of the stars, nor anything else which surpasses all understanding; you alone are a similitude of Eternal Beauty; and if you look at Him, you will become what He is, imitating Him who shines within you, whose glory is reflected in your purity. Nothing in all creation can equal your grandeur. All the heavens can fit in the palm of God's hand. . .and though He is so great. . . . you can wholly embrace Him: He dwells within you. . . .He pervades your entire being. . . .

When our human nature lay fallen upon the earth, it looked toward the serpent and held its image. But now it has arisen and looks toward the Good, turning its back on sin, it takes on the form of the Good toward which it faces. For it looks now upon the Archetypal Beauty—for that is the Dove. For turning toward the Image of Light, and within this Light, it has been made into the image of Light, and within this light it has taken the lovely form of the Dove—I mean the Dove that symbolizes the presence of the Holy Spirit. [On the Song of Songs]

This is also the teaching of the saintly Egyptian, Macarius, in the fourth century.

When God created Adam he did not give him bodily wings like a bird, but prepared for him. . . .the wings of the Holy Spirit. . . .to lift him up and carry him wherever the Spirit wishes. Saintly souls receive these wings even now. . . .[they] live in a different world; they have a table that belongs to them alone, a delight, a communion, a way of thinking uniquely theirs. This is why they are the strongest of people. They receive this strength in their souls from the Holy Spirit. . . .Thus it is possible to taste. . . .the grace of God. . . .This tasting is the dynamic power of the Spirit manifesting itself in full certitude in the heart. The sons of light. . . .have nothing to learn from man; they are taught of God. Grace itself engraves the laws of the Spirit on their hearts. . . .[and] penetrates all the members of the body. [Spiritual Homilies]

And it is the witness of the eleventh century Byzantine, St. Simeon, the New Theologian.

The only thing that God demands of us, mortals, is that we do not sin. But this. . . .is merely keeping inviolate the image and high rank which we possess by nature. Clothed thus in the radiant garment of the Spirit, we abide in God, and He in us. Through grace we become gods and sons of God and are illumined by the light of His knowledge. . .

. . . .if a man does not receive the grace of the Holy Spirit and does not see it and sense it in his soul, he is still imperfect and is an object of pity. . . .

. . . .can he who has in his heart the Divine Fire of the Holy Spirit burning naked not be set on fire, not shine and glow and take on the radiance of God. . . .through grace a man becomes wholly god. [*Theological and Practical Precepts*]

The nineteenth century Russian, St. Seraphim of Sarov, repeats the very same teaching:

Without the Holy Spirit there is not and cannot be any salvation, as it is written:
"By the Holy Spirit,
Every soul is made alive.
And is exalted in purity.
And is illumined by the Trinitarian Unity,
In the Sacred Mystery. [*Matins Hymn of the Orthodox Church*]

The Holy Spirit himself enters our souls and this entrance into our souls of Him, the Almighty, and this presence with our spirit of the Triune Majesty, is only granted to us through our own assiduous acquisition of the Holy Spirit which prepares in our souls and bodies a throne for the all-creative presence of God with our spirit, according to His irrevocable word: I will live in them and dwell in them and walk in them; and I will be their God, and they will be My People. [*Conversation with Motovilov*]

And this too is the doctrine of the peasant monk who died on Mount Athos in 1938, the holy Starez Silouan, who wrote his thoughts on scraps of paper with a simplicity and daring possible only to one filled with the Spirit of God.

Behold, a wondrous thing: a grace gave me to know that all men who love God and keep His commandments are filled with light and are in the likeness of the Lord; while those who go against God are full of darkness and are in the likeness of the enemy [i.e. the devil]. And this is natural. The Lord is Light, and He enlightens His servants, but they who serve the enemy have accepted the darkness of the enemy.

Man is made of the dust of the earth but God so loved him that he adorned him with His grace and fashioned him in the likeness of the Lord. It is said that because of our pride so few of us know this. . . .

Man was formed of the dust of the ground—what good thing can there be in him? Behold, God in His goodness adorned man with the grace of the Holy Spirit, and he became after the likeness of Jesus Christ, Son of God.

Great is this mystery, and great is the mercy of God towards man. If all the peoples of the earth knew how deeply the Lord loves man their hearts would be filled with the love of Christ and Christ's humility, and they would seek to be like Him in all things. But man cannot do this by himself, for it is only in the Holy Spirit that he can become like unto Christ. Man that is fallen purifies himself through repentance; and is made new by the grace of the Holy Spirit, and in all things becomes like unto the Lord. [Wisdom From Mount Athos. The Writings of Startez Siluoan 1866-1938]

These sayings of the saints are elaborations of the fundamental biblical doctrine that man without God is not man, but a beast, an animal bound to his carnal and biological existence, devoid of divine being and life.

"For I am the LORD your God; consecrate yourselves therefore, and be holy, for I am holy. [Leviticus 11:44]

As obedient children, do not be conformed to the passions of your former ignorance, but as he who has called you is holy, be holy yourselves in all your conduct: since it is written; "You shall be holy, for I am holy. [1 Peter 1: 14-16]

His divine power has granted to us all things that pertain to life and godliness, through the knowledge of him who called us to his own glory and excellence, by which he has granted to us his precious and very great promises, that through these you may escape from the corruption that is in the world because of passion, and become partakers of the divine nature. [2 Peter 1: 3-4]

To become partakers of the nature of God and so to be holy as God is holy is the task and goal of all human beings created in the image and likeness of God. This is accomplished only by the Spirit of God, given to man in creation and renewed in divine salvation and deification by Jesus Christ, the perfect man, the uncreated, divine, and eternal image of God, who has come "for us men and for our salvation" in human flesh. All of man's life consists in this: *to acquire the Spirit of God.*

For those who live according to the flesh set their minds on the things of the flesh, but those who live according to the Spirit set their minds on the things of the Spirit. To set the mind on the flesh is death, but to set the mind on the Spirit is life and peace. For the mind that is set on the flesh is hostile to God; it does not submit to God's law, indeed it cannot; and those who are in the flesh cannot please God. . . .for if you live according to the flesh you will die, but if by the Spirit you put to death the deeds of the body you will live. For all who are led by the Spirit of God are sons of God. [Romans 8:5-7, 13-14]

The purpose of this book is to "set our minds on the things of the Spirit" as they are shown to us from within the experience of the Eastern Orthodox Church. We hope this writing will inspire readers to seek personal contact with the sources, for we will do no more than introduce a witness to the Spirit of God given by those who have claimed his divine inspiration in Christ and the life of the catholic church.

. . . .as it is written,
"What no eye has seen,
nor ear heard,
nor the heart of man conceived, what God has prepared for those who love him,"
God has revealed to us through the Spirit. . . . now we have received not the spirit of the world, but the spirit which is from God, that we might understand the gifts bestowed on us by God. And we impart this in words not taught by human wisdom but taught by the Spirit. [1 Corinthians 2: 9-13]

Table of Contents

CHAPTER I

THE SPIRIT OF GOD

The Holy Spirit is the Spirit of God. We must never forget this—and it is easy to forget. How often, indeed, do we speak of God's Spirit as if he were ours, to be what we want him to be, to do with him what we want. But the Spirit is God's; he is our Master and Teacher, our "Lord and Giver of Life." (Nicene Creed)

God would not be God if he were devoid of his Spirit. Sometimes men think that God himself is simply the Spirit, and that the Spirit is simply God. According to the Scriptures and the testimony of the saints, this is a terrible mistake. There is in reality a radical, personal distinction between God and his Spirit, which should never be erased or confused. The Spirit is not simply God. He is the Spirit *of* God.

God in his uncreated being and life has within him by nature his Son and his Spirit, who are personally other than he. In theological terms, this is the doctrine of the Holy Trinity. It is the doctrine of the Bible and the Church, carefully formulated by the Christian fathers and teachers, but not invented or created by them. It is the doctrine of God revealed by himself in his dealings with men in their creation and salvation by the Word and the Spirit.

According to the Scriptures, God acts toward the world in his Son and his Spirit, called by St. Irenaeus, the hands of the Father. The divine Son is also called the Word and Image of God. It is he who is the eternal pattern of the spiritual being of man; the one, in, for, and through whom all things are made: the one who reveals God in the Law and the prophets; the one who is incarnate in human flesh as Jesus of Nazareth, the Messiah of Israel and the Savior of the world.

In the beginning was the Word,
And the Word was with God,
And the Word was God.
He was in the beginning with God.
All things were made through him, and
    without him was not anything made that was made.
In him was life, and the life was the light of men. . . .

And the Word became flesh and dwelt among us,
    full of grace and truth;
we have beheld his glory, glory as of the only-begotten
    Son from the Father. . . .

And from His fulness have we all received, grace upon grace
For the law was given through Moses; grace and truth came through
Jesus Christ
No one has ever seen God; the only-begotten Son, who is in the
    bosom of the Father,
he has made him known. [John 1:1-18]

The Word of God is uncreated, eternal, and divine. He is always with God, in his "bosom," as his only-begotten Son. He coexists with the Father from all eternity as the perfect reflection of the Father's glory, the "express image of his divine person." (Cf. Hebrews 1:3) He is the one in whom the entire fulness of the being and life of God is divinely and perfectly realized. He is the one who, in his incarnation as a real human being, brings to the world all the fulness of God in human form. (Cf. Colossians 1:19, 2:9; Philippians 2:5) He is the one who through his death and resurrection enables man to be the "dwelling place of God in the Spirit." (Ephesians 2:22)

The Spirit of God exists eternally with the Father and the Son. He is what God is, possessing from all eternity the fulness of divine being and life with the Father and the Son, The Spirit of God is not simply God. He is the Spirit of God who proceeds from the Father and rests in the Son. He is not an impersonal energy of God or some sort of "power of goodness" or "power of life"—whatever that may mean. Anything spiritual has to be "someone," a "who," and not simply a "what." The Spirit of God is not a vague, illusive, abstract power or force. He is the personal Spirit of the Father who shares the identical divine being and life with the Father and the Son. He is the one by whose power God creates through his Word. He seals the divine image and likeness in man and is himself the seal of God's image in man. He effects the revelation of God through his Word in the Law and the prophets. He enables the incarnation of God's Word and Son in human flesh from the Virgin. He rests and remains on Jesus, the incarnate Word, manifesting him in human form as the Christ, the Messiah of Israel. He is the one by whose power Christ "tramples down death by death" in the pascha of his crucifixion and resurrection. He dwells in those who belong to Christ, bringing to them both the Father and the Son—and the whole Kingdom of Heaven—making them to be "filled with all the fulness of God." (Cf. John 14:23, Ephesians 3:19)

According to the Scriptures and the doctrine of the Orthodox Church, the Holy Spirit, in his divine being and life, proceeds from God the Father alone, and not from the Father "and the Son" (filioque) as confessed in the creeds of the Western Christian churches. Some people think that this difference in the confession of faith about the Holy Spirit and the Trinitarian Godhead is an "abstraction" not to be dealt with seriously, a small matter interesting only to scholars and devotees of abstract theological debates.

Some say "Who knows from whom the Holy Spirit proceeds?" And others say, "Who cares, as long as he proceeds!" But in the traditional Christian view, such an attitude is not only unworthy of humans, it is disrespectful and even blasphemous toward God.

God has revealed himself. He has come and saved us. He has manifested himself to us—in his Son and his Spirit. He has given his Son and his Spirit to be with us and dwell in us. He has made himself known to us in our worthiness and sin. This is what believers proclaim in their first words of entrance into communion with God in the church on the day of their baptism:

Great are Thou, O Lord, and marvelous are Thy works, and there is no word which suffices to hymn Thy wonders. For thou, of Thine own good will has brought into being all things which before were not. . . .For Thou, O God, who art inexpressible, existing before the ages and ineffable, didst descend on earth, didst take on the form of a servant, and wast made in the likeness of man; for, because of Thy tender compassion of Thy mercy, O Master,. . . .Thou didst come and Thou didst save us. We confess Thy grace. We proclaim Thy mercy. We conceal not Thy gracious acts. Thou didst redeem the generation of our mortal nature. By Thy birth, Thou didst sanctify the virgin's womb. All creation magnifieth Thee, Who hast manifested Thyself. [First Prayer of the Orthodox Baptismal Liturgy]

We must love and honor God in his exceedingly great mercy to us. We must receive what he has given and understand what he has revealed for our wisdom and knowledge, for our understanding and enlightment, for our growth and development as creatures made in the image and likeness of God with the vocation and command to become divine by grace. It is the Orthodox conviction that in Christ and the Church men can be in communion with the mysterious being of God, becoming "partakers of the divine nature" (2 Peter 1:4), with genuine insight into the "mystery of Christ. . . . as it has now been revealed to his holy apostles and prophets by the Spirit. . . ; the mystery wisdom of God. . . that through the Church the manifold wisdom of God might be made known. . . ." (Ephesians 3:4-5, 9-10) Thus, it is no small thing to discern the true character of the Trinitarian being of God. For indeed, what can be more important to man than to have a proper vision of the nature of God, as much as it is possible, through communion with God in faith and love, as God has given such gracious communion in his Son and his Spirit?

According to the Orthodox faith, the Holy Spirit proceeds from God the Father alone, and not from the Father "and the Son" even as if "from one source."

But when the Counselor comes, whom I shall send to you from the Father, even the Spirit of truth, who proceeds from the Father, he will bear witness to me. . . . [John 15 : 26]

But the Counselor, the Holy Spirit, whom the Father will send in my name, he will teach you all the things, and bring to your remembrance all that I have said to you. [John 14 : 26]

When the Spirit of truth comes, he will guide you into all the truth. . . . [John 16 : 13]

According to the saints, one of the truths that the Spirit of truth reveals is his own divinity and that of the Son, thus showing the proper relationship between the Persons of the Holy Trinity, and their relationship to humanity and the world. (Cf. Gregory the Theologian, *Fifth Theological Oration, On the Holy Spirit.*) What one comes to know in the Spirit is that the one true and living God is the one God of Israel, the God of Abraham, Isaac, and Jacob. He alone is the "one God, the Father Almighty, Maker of heaven and earth" in whom Christians believe. (Nicene Creed)

This one, true, and living God is manifested through his Son by his Spirit as the unique source of all that exists—including the Son and the Spirit themselves, who are not "creatures," but who, necessarily and essentially, share the same divine being and life of the Father himself. This means, according to the Orthodox faith, that God would not be God without his Son and his Spirit. He would not be perfect, complete, and divine without them. He would not be the true God.

This is a crucial revelation about God and the character of his divine reality, being, and life, because it tells us that God is not and could not be God "all by himself." It tells us that God would not be the superabundant, supra-essential perfection of virtue and life —that he would not be love—if he were alone in his divinity.

In the view of the Christian Scripture and saints, a monad God is not a God at all. A uni-personal deity is no deity; it is not perfect and divine. By God's own report, a one-person God would not and could not be divine and complete. He would be absolutely alone, absolutely isolated, absolutely self-centered, absolutely locked up in the bounds of his own "perfection"—which would, thereby, not be "perfection" at all.

The perfect God shows us, in his self-manifestation by his Word and Spirit, that his divine nature is essentially self-communicating, self-expressing, and self-sharing. The essential self-communication and self-expression of God results in the eternal existence of God's divine Son—his Word and Image—and God's Holy Spirit. Both are divinely perfect, for both are identically and exactly *what* God the Father is, yet are not *who* He is, being *personally* distinct. This is the meaning of the term "consubstantial" (or "of one essence"—homo-ousios) in the church's creedal confession about the only-begotten Son and the life creating Spirit. The Son and the Spirit are not "creatures." They are essentially and eternally divine with the Father. They are exactly and identically what the Father is. But they are not the Father himself.

The Spirit of God, in his own unique and personal "mode of existence" (St. Basil's expression), is distinct from God the Father and the Son in that the Spirit is the divine person who "proceeds from the Father," in a manner similar to the "eternal generation" of the Son from the Father, but not the same, because he is God's Spirit and not God's Son. St. Gregory the Theologian makes this point quite clearly. The person of the Son is uniquely the "express image" of the Father's hypostasis (his divine person), (Cf. Hebrews 1:3). And the person of the Holy Spirit is the one whose divine "mode of existence" is to be God's living and personal Spirit—and not his Son.

The Spirit of God exists eternally as the the divine person, one of the Holy Trinity, to be the hypostatic realization of the living character of God the Father, the One who personally expresses and communicates the infinite and innumerable multiplicity of divine activities and energies which belong to God's supra-essential, superabundantly inexhaustible pleroma of being and life, which is wholly and perfectly "imaged" and "contained" in the person of the Son. The Holy Spirit, therefore, does not and cannot possibly proceed from the Father "and the Son." He must proceed from the Father alone as the Scripture says, the Father who is alone the unique "source of divinity" (*principium divinitatis*] of both the Son and the Holy Spirit.

It is important for us to see this and to confess it plainly. Man's proper vision of the triune God demands it. For as St. Athanasius has said, the true and living God is the Father alone. The personal divine realization of the Father is the Son—the truth and the life, "who for us men and for our salvation. . . was incarnate by the Holy Spirit of the Virgin Mary, And was made man." (Nicene Creed) And the Holy Spirit is the personal Spirit of Truth, the Spirit of Life, the "Lord, and Giver of Life, Who proceedeth from the Father" (Nicene Creed) and who, through Christ, fills all creation with all the fulness of God. It is exactly about this that the faithful sing on the great and final feast of Pentecost in the church; the day when the Spirit of God comes to make all people children of God the Father through His Son Jesus Christ:

The Holy Spirit has ever been,
Is and always will be.
For He is wholly without beginning and end.
Yet He is in union with the Father and the Son.
Life and Life-Giver,
Light and Light-Giver.
Good by nature and the Fountain of Goodness.
Through Whom the Father is known and the Son is glorified.
And by all it is understood that One Power, One Rank,
One Worship are of the Holy Trinity.

Light, Life and A Living Supersensible Fountain is the Holy Spirit.
Good, Upright, Supersensible Spirit of Understanding.

Presiding and Purifying.
Divine and Deifying.
Fire projecting from Fire.
Speaking, Active, Distributor of Gifts.
Through Whom all of the prophets, apostles and martyrs are
crowned.
A Strange Report:
A Strange Sight:
A Fire divided for the distribution of gifts. [*Vesper Hymns of*
Pentecost]

Sometimes, it is said that God is the Father, God is the Son, and God is the Holy Spirit. Wrongly understood—as it often is—this is misleading and inaccurate. It gives the impression that there is one God who is Father, Son, and Holy Spirit, either at one and the same time; or even worse, successively and at different times; or worse yet, merely in appearance in his action toward men and the world. The impression is that there is but one God who somehow expresses himself in three different forms, but who "in himself" is one. It is an attempt to save the divine unity, while being faithful to the "revelation" of the Trinity. (Cf. St. Augustine, *On The Trinity*) This well-meant attempt is fundamentally wrong and has caused great damage to man's vision of God and all reality in him, not to mention great division among Christians.

The one God of faith is God the Father. There is one God because there is one Father, says St. Gregory the Theologian. And this one God is perfect and divine, true and living, Love itself, because he has with him by nature his only-begotten Son and his most Holy Spirit. Through the Son (begotten of the Father) and the Spirit (proceeding from the Father) the one true God is shown to be and becomes the Father of men, who address him as Abba!

. . .we were slaves to the elemental spirits of the universe. But when
the time had fully come, God sent forth his Son, born of
woman. . . .so that we might be made sons. And because you are
sons, God has sent the Spirit of His Son into our hearts, crying,

"Abba! Father!" [*Galatians 4:3-6*]

So God is not a sterile monad, an abstract essence, an impersonal absolute, a unipersonal substance, a chief spirit among many spirits, a supreme being in a long chain of beings, He is not "one God manifested as Trinity." He is—supra-essentially and super-abundantly, beyond human comprehension—God the Father who is love, who through the "Son of his love" (Colossians 1:13) pours his love into our hearts through the Holy Spirit who has been given to us. (Romans 5:5)

This is what the Spirit himself manifests to us in the life of the church. It is the knowledge of God for which we were created. For to refer to St. Athanasius once more:

For what profit is it to creatures if they did not know their Creator? Or how could they be rational without knowing the Father's Word in Whom they received their very being? For there would be nothing to distinguish them from brute creatures if they had knowledge of nothing but earthly things. No, why did God make them at all if He did not wish to be known by them? For this, lest it should be so, being good, He gives them a share in His own Image, our Lord Jesus Christ, and makes them after His likeness, so that by grace, [of the Spirit], perceiving the Image, that is, the Word of the Father, they may be able through Him to know the Father, and knowing their Maker, live the happy and truly blessed life. [On the Incarnation of the Word of God]

So it is that we have the knowledge of God, whom no one has ever seen, or can see, shining from the face of Christ in the Holy Spirit.

And we all, with unveiled faces, beholding the glory of the Lord, are being changed into His likeness from one degree of glory to another; for this comes from the Lord, Who is the Spirit.

For it is God who said, "Let light shine out of darkness," Who has shone in our hearts to give the light of the knowledge of the glory of God in the face of Christ. [*2 Corinthians 3:18; 4:6*]

It is in the person of Christ, the incarnate Son of God, that the Spirit of God who proceeds from the Father is most fully revealed.

CHAPTER II

THE SPIRIT OF CHRIST

Jesus of Nazareth, the Son of God in human flesh, is the anointed holy one of God, the Messiah of Israel, the Lord and Savior of the world, because the Spirit of the Lord is upon him:

The Spirit of the Lord is upon me, because he has anointed me to preach good news to the poor.
He has sent me to proclaim release to the captives
and recovering of sight to the blind, to set at liberty those who are oppressed,
to proclaim the acceptable year of the Lord. [Luke 4:18-19, Cf Isaiah 61:1-2]

Behold, my servant, Whom I uphold, my chosen, in Whom my soul delights; I have put my Spirit upon Him, He will bring forth justice to the nations. . . .and in his name will the Gentiles hope. [Isaiah 42:1-4, Matthew 12:18-21]

There shall come forth a shoot from the stump of Jesse,
and a branch shall grow out of his roots.
And the Spirit of the LORD shall rest upon him,
the spirit of wisdom and understanding,
the spirit of counsel and might,
the spirit of knowledge and the fear of the LORD.
And his delight shall be in the fear of the LORD. [Isaiah 11:1-3]

The Son of God becomes human that for our salvation he might be the anointed one upon whom the Spirit of God rests and remains forever. The Fathers of the Church say this in many ways. St. Athanasius is very explicit. All that Christ is and all that he does as a man, he is and he does *for us*.

He is anointed here not that He may become God,
for He was so even before. . . .but in our behalf.

. . . .being God, and ever ruling in the Father's kingdom, and being Himself He who supplies the Holy Spirit, nevertheless is here said to be anointed, that, as before, being said as man to be anointed with the Spirit, He might provide for us men, not only exaltation and resurrection, but the indwelling and intimacy with the Holy Spirit.

. . . .when he is anointed. . . .we it is who in Him are anointed. . . .when He is baptized, we it is who in Him are baptized. . . .Because of us, He asked for glory. . . that we might take and to us be given, and we might be exalted in Him; as also He consecrates Himself, that we might be consecrated in Him [Oration IV, Against the Arians]

In his mystical writings, St. Gregory of Nyssa says the same thing:

And He Himself [Christ] received this glory [of God the Father] when He put on human nature, though He had indeed always possessed it since before the foundation of the world. And now that His human nature has been glorified by the Spirit it is communicated to all who are united with Him, beginning with His disciples. [Commentary on the Canticle of Canticles]

As man, for us men and for our salvation, the incarnate Word of God "recapitulates" (the favorite word of St. Irenaeus) all that belongs to humanity, and even man's sin, his curse and his death, so that, experiencing everything that belongs to fallen humanity, he might purify and heal all of man's life and redirect his existence toward God, in communion with him in the Spirit.

Christ redeemed us from the curse of the law, having become a curse for us. . . .that in Christ Jesus the blessing of Abraham might come upon the Gentiles, that we might receive the promise of the Spirit through faith. [Galatians 3:13-14]

For God has done what the law. . .could not do: sending his own Son in the likeness of sinful flesh and for sin, he condemned sin in the flesh, in order that the just requirement of the law might be fulfilled in us, who walk not according to the flesh but according to the Spirit. [Romans 8:3-4]

But we see Jesus, who for a little while was made lower than the angels, crowned with glory and honor because of the suffering of death, so that by the grace of God he might taste death for every one. . . .Since therefore the children share in flesh and blood, he himself likewise partook of the same nature, that through death he might destroy him who has the power of death, that is, the devil. . . .Therefore he had to be made like his brethren in every aspect. . . .to make expiation for the sins of the people. [Hebrews 2:9, 14, 17]

St. John Chrysostom, commenting on the fact that for our salvation Christ Jesus who was "in the form of God. . . .emptied himself, taking the form of a servant, being born in the likeness of men. . . .humbled himself and became obedient to death, even death on a cross" (Philippians 2:6-8), says simply that Christ has done for use everything that can possibly be done. In love with creation, his adulterous bride, as a passionate young lover, Chrysostom says, the Son of God pursued her and sought her and followed her to where she was. He even became what she was—sinful, cursed, and dead—in order to win her by his love and take her home to the house of his Father, purified and cleansed, and made splendid in the beauty of his own divinity. He accomplished his mission. He redeemed his beloved. He adorned his "harlot bride" with the majestic glory of his own perfection, filling her with all the fulness of God by the indwelling of the Spirit. St. Gregory the Theologian taught exactly the same thing when he said simply: "What is not assumed has not been healed." (Letter 101; *To Cledonius*] But Christ assumed everything and healed all by the grace of the Spirit of God.

The Spirit of God is Christ's own Spirit. It is his to have and his to give. He has received the Spirit from God the Father. It is his not merely as the divine Son of God; it is his as a man, as Jesus of Nazareth, as the "one of us" whom he has become in order to bestow the Spirit upon us.

Human beings must have the Spirit of God in order to live, to love, to know the truth, and to conquer their sinful passions. They must have the Spirit to fulfill themselves as the creatures made in the image and likeness of God to be filled with all the fulness of God for an eternity of everlasting life. But fallen humanity does not have the Spirit. This is the meaning of "Adam's sin." Human beings lose the Spirit through sin. They quench the Spirit in them from God by enslaving themselves to "this world" through "the lust of the flesh and the lust of the eyes and the pride of life." (1 John 2:16) Jesus therefore comes as the new and final Adam—for the original Adam was himself but a "a type of the one who was to come," the Lord Jesus Christ. (Romans 5:14)

"The first man Adam became a living being; the last Adam became a life-giving spirit. . . . The first man was from the earth, a man of dust; the second man is from heaven. As was the man of dust, so are those who are of the dust; and as is the man of heaven; so are those who are of heaven. Just as we have borne the image of the man of dust, we shall also bear the image of the man of heaven.
[*1 Corinthians 15:45, 47-49*]

We bear the image of the "man of heaven" and are ourselves "of heaven"—as the fathers say, we are ourselves *made heaven*—when we are one with Christ, the eternal Bridegroom, and receive from him the Spirit of God.

When we are "in Christ" (St. Paul's expression), we share Christ's being and life, which is the being and life of God himself in human form. And sharing Christ's divine humanity we are empowered by God's Spirit to do the works that Christ does; and even "greater works," for we are left in this world as he returns to the Father.

Truly, truly, I say to you, he who believes in me will also do the works that I do; and greater works than these will he do, because I go to the Father. Whatever you ask in my name, I will do it, that the Father may be glorified in the Son; if you ask anything in my name, I will do it. [John 14:12-14]

These are certainly among the most shocking words in the Scriptures: "greater works than these will he do. . . ." But they are spoken by the Word Incarnate to those who will become "divine by grace" through his Holy Spirit. As Christ's disciples, his brothers and sisters according to our humanity, his faithful friends, his beloved bride, his spiritual body, his extending branches, his living stones—all scriptural images of our relationship to him—we are enabled to be what he is and to do what he has done by the grace of his power. This is why he came to us and breathed God's Holy Spirit upon us.

The main characteristic of being like Christ and doing what he does is to know him as the truth, to live with him as the life, to follow him as the way, and so to love God and man and all of creation with the very same love with which he has loved and continues to love, which is the Love of God.

. . .we have peace with God through our Lord Jesus Christ. Through him we have obtained access to this grace in which we stand, and we rejoice in our hope of sharing the glory of God. More than that, we rejoice in our sufferings, knowing that suffering produces endurances and endurance produces character, and character produces hope, and hope does not disappoint us, because God's love has been poured into our hearts through the Holy Spirit which has been given to us. [Romans 5:1-5]

It may be claimed that Christ taught nothing which was not already taught in the Scriptures of the Old Testament. It is certainly proclaimed that Jesus himself fulfilled all that the Old Testament, in the Law and the prophets, foretold and commanded. Christ alone, of all men, has lived in human form as the image of God. He alone has reflected fully in His humanity all the fulness of God in his earthly life. He alone has loved the Lord his God with all his heart, with all his soul, with all his mind, and with all his strength; and has loved his neighbor—and even his enemy—as himself, in perfect humility, meekness, purity, and self-sacrifice. He alone has done the will of God by identifying himself fully and totally with the least of God's creatures: the hungry, the thirsty, naked, estranged, wounded, and imprisoned. For being himself hungry, thirsty, naked, estranged, wounded, and imprisoned, he has become for all who are in these conditions—and we all are—the bread of life, the living water, the garments of salvation, the house of the Father, the healing of infirmities, and the liberation from all bondage. (Cf. Matthew 23:37-38, 25:31 ff) Christ has done it all, and is All. (Cf. Colossians 3:11) On the cross all is fulfilled. (John 19:30) And so in the Holy Spirit he commands all people to fulfill their lives as he has fulfilled his, to continue in his word, to walk in his way, to follow his truth, to live with his life, and finally and most fully, to love with the same love with which he has loved: the love of God.

A new commandment I give to you, that you love one another; even as I have loved you, that you also love one another. [John 15:12]

This is my commandment, that you love one another as I have loved you. [John 15:12]

"Even as I have loved you." This is the central element and the whole importance of the "new commandment" given by Christ to his people. It is accomplished by the fulfillment of perfect identification in love with all people, "with the least of the brethren," and so with Christ himself. Such "identification" comes only when men are filled with the Spirit of God.

Beloved, let us love one another; for love is of God, and he who

.*loves is born of God and knows God. He who does not love does not .
know God; for God is love. In this the love of God was made
manifest among us, that God sent his only Son into the world, so
that we might live through him. In this is love, not that we moved
God but that he loved us and sent his Son to be the expiation for our
sins. Beloved, if God so loved us, we also ought to love one another.
No man has ever seen God; if we love one another, God abides in us
and his love is perfected in us. By this we know that we abide in him
and he in us, because he has given us of his own Spirit.* [1 John
4:7-13]

CHAPTER III

THE SPIRIT IN THE CHURCH

God gives His Holy Spirit to man personally in the life of the Christian Church. The Church itself is nothing other than life in the Holy Spirit, life lived in communion with God through Christ by the grace and power of the Spirit of God. It is human life as God originally intended it to be.

Father Sergius Bulgakov, the well-known Russian émigré theologian, begins his book *The Orthodox Church*, with the following words:

Orthodoxy is the Church of Christ on earth. The Church of Christ is not an institution; it is new life with Christ and in Christ, guided by the Holy Spirit. Christ, the Son of God, came to earth, was made man, uniting His divine life with that of humanity.

The Church, in her quality of Body of Christ, which lives with the life of Christ, is by that fact the domain where the Holy Spirit lives and works. More: The Church is life by the Holy Spirit because it is the Body of Christ. This is why the Church may be considered as a blessed life in the Holy Spirit, or the life of the Holy Spirit in humanity.

Written forty years ago, these words of Father Bulgakov express no new doctrine of the Church, no new and modern vision or version of the Christian faith. Indeed, the Russian theologian says nothing different, in essence, from what was written in the book of Deuteronomy centuries ago.

Hear, O Israel: The Lord our God is one Lord; and you shall love the Lord your God with all your heart, with all your mind, with all your soul, with all your might. And these words which I command you this day should be written upon your heart; and you shall teach them diligently to your children, and shall talk of them when you sit in your house, and when you walk by the way, and when you lie down, and when you rise. . . . For you are a people holy to the Lord your God; the Lord your God has chosen you to be a people of His possession. . . . You shall therefore love the Lord your God; and keep His charge, his statutes and His ordinances and his commandments always. . . . For this commandment which I command you this day is not too hard for you, neither is it far off. It is not in heaven, that you should say, "Who will bring it down to us. . . ." Neither is it beyond the sea, that you should say, "Who will. . . bring it to us. . . ?" But the Word is very near you; it is in your mouth and in your heart, so that you can do it. [Deuteronomy, 6:4-7; 7:6; 30:11-14]

What is this teaching, if not "the life of the Holy Spirit in humanity"? What is it, if not God indwelling in man by his Word made present and active in man's life by the Spirit of God? Even the life of the Old Covenant, of Israel according to the flesh, the life of God's people living by God's Law, is life in communion with the holiness of God himself: "For I am the Lord your God; consecrate yourself, therefore, and be holy, for I am holy." (Leviticus 11:44)

Thus, as the apostle Paul has said, the Law of God is "spiritual." It is "holy and just and good." It is "the embodiment of knowledge and truth." (Romans 2:20, 7:12-14) Man's failure to fulfill the Law has convinced him of his weakness and sin—but it has not altered the fact that his life consists in sharing the holiness of God in his own being and life. Thus, with the Law as "tutor," man has come to know that the fulness and perfection of life in union with God is given by God's grace in Jesus Christ, and that, by the grace of God's Spirit in Christ, man can "come to fulness of life in him." (Colossians 2 : 10)

This is the teaching not only of the New Testament Church, but of the prophets of the Old Covenant as well. For it was written long before Christ's coming that the Lord would establish a new and final covenant with man.

A new heart I will give you, and a new spirit I will put within you; and I will take out of your flesh the heart of stone and give you a heart of flesh. And I will put my spirit within you, and cause you to walk in my statutes and be careful to observe my ordinances. [Ezekiel 36 : 26-27]

. . . I will put my law within them, and I will write it upon their hearts, and I will be their God, and they will be my people. And no longer shall each teach his brother, saying, "Know the LORD," for they shall all know me, from the least to the greatest, says the Lord; for I will forgive their iniquity and I will remember their sin no more. [Jeremiah 31 : 33-34]

This is what is fulfilled in the Church of the risen Christ. This is what is given in the New Covenant community of life in God's Messiah. This is what happens in the "last days" when God pours out his own Holy Spirit on people of all nations. This was spoken of by the prophet Joel and witnessed by the apostle Peter on the day of Pentecost. This is what is proclaimed and testified to in the Church by the apostles Paul and John :

. . . you are a letter from Christ delivered by us, written not with ink, but with the Spirit of the Living God, not on tablets of stone, but on tablets of human hearts. Such is the confidence that we have through Christ toward God. . . Who has qualified us to be ministers of a new covenant, not in a written code but in the Spirit; for the written code kills, but the Spirit gives life [2 Corinthians 3 : 3-4].

But you have been anointed by the Holy One, and you know everything. . . . the anointing which you received from him abides in you, and you have no need that any one should teach you; as his anointing teaches you about everything, and is true. . . . .All who keep his commandments abide in him, and he in them. And by this we know that he abides in us, by the Spirit which he has given us. [1 John 2:20, 26; 3:24]

Thus, Father Bulgakov's doctrine is the doctrine of God's prophets and apostles. It is also the doctrine of the fathers and saints of the Church. For, as Saint Irenaeus has said it most simply, we have the "firm belief in the Spirit of God who furnishes us with a knowledge of the truth and has set forth the dispensations of the Father and the Son, in virtue of which He dwells with every generation of men, according to the will of the Father. True knowledge is the doctrine of the apostles and the ancient character of the Church throughout the world. . . . For where the church is, there is the Spirit of God, and where the Spirit of God is, there is the Church and the fulness of grace." (*Against the Heresies*)

Against all falsehood, ignorance, and perversion of men's minds, the holy fathers of the faith present the life and teaching of the "catholic church." The term "catholic" does not mean, in the language of the church fathers, the "universal" church, or the church "throughout all parts of the world." It means rather the Church as full, complete, whole, lacking nothing of the fulness of God and his Kingdom. The term "catholic" is a qualitiative, not a quantitative adjective describing the reality and character of the Church. It is the traditional description for the Church, found first in the early second century writings of Saint Ignatius of Antioch. It expresses what the letter to the Ephesians claims when it says that God has put all things under the feet of Christ and "has made him who fills all in all." (Ephesians 1:22-23)

The "whole fulness of deity" is in Christ "bodily," for "in him all the fulness of God was pleased to dwell." (Colossians 2:9, 1:19) In him we have all come "to fulness of life," for he, being the incarnate life and light of God—and of every man and all creation—has come in the flesh "full of grace and truth," that "of his fulness" we may all receive "grace upon grace." (Colossians 2:10, John 1:14-16) This gracious fulness of divine light and life, this gracious fulness of God himself, given to the world in Christ, is what his body, the catholic church, is: "the fulness of Him who fills all in all." (Ephesians 1:23)

It is in this sense that Saint Cyprian could say in the third century quite simply: "He is not a Christian who is not in the Church of Christ." (Letter 55) "He cannot have God as Father who has not the Church as Mother." (*On the Unity of the Church*) "Without the Church there is no salvation." (Letter 73) For, as Father George Florovsky says commenting on these words, *"Salvation is the Church."*[1]

This also was the teaching of Saint Athanasius in the fourth century, when he appealed to the "tradition, teaching and faith of the catholic church from the beginning, which the Lord gave, the apostles preached and the fathers kept," saying that, "upon this the Church is founded, and he who should fall away from it would not be a Christian and should no longer be so called." (*First Letter to Serapion*)

And St. Basil the Great, decrying the divisions and perversions brought by those who separated themselves into a "sect opposed to the church of God," writes in the most graphic manner about the Arian heresies:

What storm at sea was ever so fierce and wild as this present tempest. . .? In it every landmark of the Fathers has been moved, every foundation, every bulwark of opinion has been shaken. . . we see, as it were, whole churches, crew and all, shattered upon the sunken reefs of disingenuous heresies, while others, who are enemies of the Spirit of Salvation, have seized the helm and made shipwreck of the faith. . . . Between the opposing parties inspired Scripture is powerless to mediate; the tradition of apostles cannot suggest terms of arbitration. . . . Everyone is a theologian though he have his soul branded with more stains then can be counted. The result is that innovators find a plentiful source of men ripe for faction, while self-appointed scions of the house. . .reject the government of the

1. "Sobornost: The Catholicity of the Church", in *The Church of God.*

Holy Scripture. . . .[On the Holy Spirit]

Wherefore we too [like the faithful of old] are undismayed at the cloud of our enemies, and resting our hope on the aid of the Spirit have, with all boldness, proclaimed the Truth. [On the Holy Spirit]

St. Basil's brother, Saint Gregory of Nyssa, is equally bold in his assertions. He says that "the establishment of the church is a re-creation of the world." *(On the Canticle of Canticles)* And he identifies the presence of the Holy Spirit in the Church with the presence of the Kingdom of God in the midst of the earth.

The Son is King, and His living, realized and personified Kingship [or Kingdom] is found in the Holy Spirit, Who anoints the only-begotten Son and makes Him the anointed, and the King of all that exists. If, then, the Father is King and the only-begotten Son is King, and the Holy Spirit is the Kingship [or Kingdom], one and the same definition of Kingship must prevail throughout the Trinity. [On the Holy Spirit]

Father Pavel Florensky, the Russian scientific genius who died in the nineteen fifties in a Soviet camp, comments on this doctrine of St. Gregory in his still untranslated book *The Pillar and Bulwark of Truth.* The title is taken from the line in the first letter to Timothy in the New Testament which refers to the Church as "the Church of the living God, the pillar and bulwark of the Truth." (1 Timothy 3:15)

"The Kingdom of God," he [St. Paul] writes to the Romans, "is righteousness and peace and joy in the Holy Spirit."[Romans 14:17]

Divine worship and the sacraments are the external manifestations of the Kingdom of God in churchly life. . . . And we all invoke the final coming of the Kingdom—of the Holy Spirit—every day. For according to St. Gregory of Nyssa, The Lord's Prayer. . . had an important variant which does not exist in the modern text. It was read both as: "Our Father. . . The Kingdom come. . . [and] Thy Holy Spirit come upon us and cleanse us. . . ."

. . . Gregory of Nyssa concludes that there is an identity of meaning in the phrases "Holy Spirit" and "Kingdom of God," i.e. that "the Holy Spirit is the Kingdom. . . ." And later, basing his thought on this last conclusion, St. Gregory develops the remarkable doctrine of the Spirit as "the Kingdom of the Father and the Unction of the Son."

"The Anointing One is the Father, the Anointed One is the Son, and the Unction itself. . .is the Holy Spirit." [The Pillar and Bulwark of Truth]

Father Florensky then goes on to show in his original and perplexing book—his only work in theology—that such also was the doctrine of St. Irenaeus and St. Maximus the Confessor in the seventh century. And we know as well that St. Athanasius has taught a similar doctrine.

. . . being God and ever ruling in the Father's Kingdom, and being Himself He who supplies the Holy Spirit, [He] nevertheless is said to be anointed that. . . He might provide for us men, not only exaltation and resurrection, but the indwelling and intimacy of the Holy Spirit. [Oration II Against the Arians]

Being thus sealed [by the Spirit] we are duly made "partakers of the divine nature" [2 Peter 1:4]; and thus all creation partakes of the Word in the Spirit. [First Letter to Serapion]

On the basis of such a vision and experience of God through Christ in the Holy Spirit, the Church in the Eastern Orthodox tradition has come to be called the "Kingdom of God on earth." Such a title for the Church is not a reference to the churchly temple with its icons, vestments, candles, incense, singing, and liturgical "symbolism." Rather, these artistic and liturgical "externals" are the symbolic and mystical expressions of the factual reality that the Church itself is the presence of Immanuel: God with us in the final covenant community of faith in Jesus Christ, the incarnate Son and Word of God, in the Holy Spirit. They are the manifestations of the fact that indeed the Kingdom of God—the Spirit of God and of

Christ—is in the midst of us in the life of Christ's church.

Thus for the Orthodox and, we believe, for all the fathers and saints of the catholic tradition, the Church of Christ is the Kingdom of God on earth. It is the Kingdom of the Father given to man in his Son—"of whose Kingdom there will be no end" (Luke 1:33, Nicene Creed)—in the Holy Spirit. It is the Kingdom established by God, which no earthly or heavenly power can create or destroy: The Kingdom that no one can attain by his own manipulation, ingenuity, or power. The Kingdom for which the world was made, but which itself is "not of this world." (John 18:36) The Kingdom of the Blessed Trinity which has no end. The Kingdom which is "the life of the Holy Spirit in humanity"—begun now in faith, in mystery and sacrament in the covenant community of the Messiah, and still to be manifested throughout creation at the end of the ages when Christ returns in glory to judge the living and the dead.

The Church understood and experienced as God's Kingdom on earth is, therefore, no mere human institution. It is not an organization of men exercising power and authority, not even in the name of God. Such a teaching has been explicitly denied in Orthodox tradition, as the words of the Russian religious philosopher Alexei Khomiakov, which have been universally adopted by the Orthodox, bear witness:

No, the Church is not an authority, just as God is not an authority and Christ is not an authority, since authority is something external to us. The Church is not an authority, I say, but Truth—and at the same time the inner life of the Christian since God, Christ, the Church live in him with a life more real than the heart which is beating in his breast or the blood flowing through his veins. But they are alive in him only as he is living the all-embracing life of love and unity, i.e. the life of the Church. . . that free unity which is the manifestation of the Spirit of God [On the Western Confessions of Faith].

The Church is also not some sort of invisible "platonic ideal" whose reality and fulness remain remote from man and his world, devoid of concrete structures and incarnate expressions in human history. The Church is not simply a spiritual, mystical ideal, a "kingdom of heaven" to be believed in and hoped for, which remains beyond our human experience. And still less is the Church simply the company of believers called Christians, who believe "according to freedom of conscience" by exercising their "inalienable religious rights" through a multitude of conflicting and contradictory doctrines, practices, and forms of religious life.

The Church, as God's Kingdom on the earth, has a definite human form. It is present in space and time. It has a history. It can be seen and heard. It can, we might say, even be touched, tasted, and smelled. It has a definite content, a doctrinal teaching, a sacramental structure, a mystical life, all of which are the expressions of "the Holy Spirit in the life of humanity." It has an identity and continuity in the life of man, from Christ—even from Abraham—down to the present moment. It changes, has changed, and must change in its external manifestations as it moves through history, for it is a living organism, and not a "static substance," involving the interaction and cooperation of God and man. But it changes and develops only that it might remain forever exactly what it is. It changes (to use an expression of Father Alexander Schmemann of St. Vladimir's Seminary) in order that it may remain forever the same. It changes, in a word, by the Spirit of God.

The Church realizes and expresses itself in the life of man as God's covenant community through its scriptures and liturgies, its doctrines and dogmas, its councils and canons, its fathers and saints, its icons and hymns. All these are deeply and essentially interrelated and integrated in the one living reality of the theandric fulness of the Catholic Church. No one expression of the Church's being and life can be separated from any other of its expressions or else it ceases to be what it is: an expression of the Church's catholic being and life. This is especially and primarily true of the holy Scriptures, which are the Scriptures of the Church, produced in and by the Church through the inspiration of the Holy Spirit, for the edification of the Church and the instruction, correction, guidance, and inspiration of its earthly members. To tear the Bible from the total life of the Church is to do violence to the wholeness of the Church's fabric and to deform the holy writings in the process, rendering them incapable of proper interpretation and power. This is the exact teaching of the fathers and saints of the Church for whom the appreciation of the Bible as a book in itself, apart from the Church, even the book of God's holy Word, would be the greatest distortion and sacrilege.

All expressions of the Church as the Kingdom of God on earth, the "life of the Holy Spirit in humanity," are elements of a total life, expressions of God's life becoming man's through Christ and the Spirit. They must be received and lived as elements of the whole theandric life of the Catholic Church, the life (to use St. Augustine's celebrated expression) of the *Totus Christus*, the Whole Christ, Head and Body.

The expressions of the Church's being and life—the Scriptures, dogmas, sacraments, and saints—are "authorities" for the members of the Church only as they are approached and appreciated "externally," only as they are received as realities in themselves, "over" and "apart from" the life of the faithful. They cease to be authorities the moment they are embraced by the faithful and become elements of their own life in existential communion with God. They cease to be authorities the moment they are "put on" by the faithful in the same way that Christ ceases to be an external authority for human beings when, as St. Paul has said, he is "put on" through baptism: "For as many as have been baptized into Christ have put on Christ." (Galatians 3:27) For, as the apostle has also said, "When one is united to the Lord he becomes one Spirit with him." (1 Corinthians 6:17) It is the same Spirit who inspires and vivifies the Scriptures, dogmas, sacraments, and saints of the Church, who inspires and vivifies the members of the Church who are "united to the Lord" through them.

Many striking and bold witnesses to this understanding of the Church are found in the writings of the saints, as this passage from St. Simeon the New Theologian—reminiscent of the teaching of the apostles Paul and John—indicates:

. . . *a man who consciously possesses in himself God the Giver of knowledge to men, has already studied all the holy scriptures and has collected, like fruit, all the benefit their reading can afford. So he no longer has to read books. For what need can a man have to read books if he is in converse with Him Who inspired the writers of the holy scriptures and if all His ineffable mysteries are indelibly inscribed within him? On the contrary, he himself will be for others an inspired book containing mysteries both old and new, inscribed in him by the finger of God, since he has accomplished everything and in God is at rest from all works—this is the height of perfection.* [*Practical and Theological Precepts*]

This is indeed the "height of perfection," but it is also indicative of the way of "perfecting" within the life of the Church when, by gradual growth, what is given in the Church's scriptural and sacramental expressions, as well as in its doctrines and saints, is "put on" by the believer and becomes an abiding element in his or her own spiritual life.

In the Eastern Orthodox view, the holy tradition of the Church is nothing else than the life of the Spirit in the Church, in all the Church's theandric expressions, including the Scriptures, which must be put on and lived by the people of God. Holy tradition is none of the expressions of the Church taken in isolation from any other of its expressions, nor is it all of them added together. Nor is it everything in the Church's life *in addition* to the Bible. It is rather *that* of which all the Church's theandric forms—including the Bible—are manifestations, *that* to which all of the Church's human forms bear witness and lead. On this point, it is fitting to quote another great contemporary Russian theologian, Vladimir Lossky:

If the scriptures and all that the church can produce in words, written or pronounced, in images or in symbols, liturgical or otherwise, represent the differing modes of expression of the Truth, Tradition is the unique mode *of receiving it. We say specifically* unique mode *and not* uniform mode, *for to Tradition in its pure notion there belongs nothing formal. It does not impose on human consciousness formal guarantees of the truths of faith, but gives access to the discovery of their evidence. It is not the content of Revelation, but the light that reveals it: It is not the Word, but the living Breath which makes the words heard,* [being] *at the same time the Silence*

*from which it comes [cf. St. Ignatius, St. Basil]; it is not the Truth,
but a communication of the Spirit of Truth, outside of which the
Truth cannot be received.*

*The pure notion of Tradition can then be defined by saying that it is
the life of the Holy Spirit in the Church, communicating to each
member of the Body of Christ the faculty of hearing, of receiving, of
knowing the Truth in the light which belongs to it. . . .*

*It is only in the Church that one is able to recognize in full
consciousness the unity of inspiration in the sacred books [of
scripture], because the Church alone possesses the Tradition—the
knowledge in the Holy Spirit of the Incarnate Word.*

*In fact, if Tradition is the faculty of judging in the Light of the Holy
Spirit, it obliges those who wish to know the Truth in the Tradition
to make incessant efforts: one does not remain in the Tradition by a
certain historical inertia. . . by force of habit. . . .*

*One can say that Tradition represents the critical spirit of the
Church. But contrary to the "critical spirit" of human science, the
critical judgment of the Church is made acute by the Holy Spirit.*

*The dynamism of Tradition allows of no inertia either in habitual
forms of piety or in dogmatic expressions that are repeated
mechanically like magic recipes of Truth, guaranteed by the
authority of the Church. To preserve the "dogmatic Tradition" does
not mean to be attached to doctrinal formulas: to be within the
Tradition is to keep the living truth in the Light of the Holy Spirit; or
rather, it is to be kept in the Truth by the vivifying power of
Tradition. But this power, like all that comes from the Spirit,
preserves by a ceaseless renewing.* [1]

Thus, it is the Holy Spirit who makes the Church truly the
Church of Christ, ever the same yet continually changing, which

1. Vladimir Lossky, "Tradition and Traditions," in *The Image
and Likeness of God*. New York: St. Vladimir's Press, 1974.

nothing created can divide or destroy, the "Church of the living God, the pillar and bulwark of the Truth." (1 Timothy 3:15) The Church which is Christ's "body, the fulness of Him who fills all in all" (Ephesians 1:23), against which "the gates of hell shall not prevail." (Matthew 16:18) The Church that is entered, honored, served, venerated, and believed in as *one* with the unity of the triune God; the Church which is *holy* with the holiness of its thrice-holy Lord; the Church which is *catholic* with the pleroma of divine being and life; the Church which is *apostolic* by being sent into the world as its Head himself has been sent by the Father, and as he has sent his apostles, full of grace and truth, that through him all people might "have life and have it abundantly" in eternal communion with God in the Spirit. (Cf. John 10:10)

Thus, the Church is not an authoritarian earthly institution existing by divine right and possessing divine doctrines and sacraments, decreed and implemented by divinely appointed potentates. Nor is the Church a free charismatic society of believers preaching divine doctrines and celebrating divine mysteries without visible hierarchal structures or traditional sacramental forms. The Church is rather the life of the Holy Spirit in humanity in God's new and final covenant community in the Messiah, which has a definite doctrinal teaching and a concrete sacramental form in space and time, which are preserved by the Spirit of God who lives within the Body and perpetually guarantees access to God the Father through his Son Jesus Christ.

CHAPTER IV

THE SPIRIT
IN THE SACRAMENTS

The earthly form and structure of the Church of Christ is sacramental, or in the language of the Eastern Church, it is "mystical." One finds the Church in human history as the sacramental, mystical body of Christ. The official expression of the Church in the world is its liturgical gathering. When the Church gathers in Christ in the presence of the Father by the grace of the Spirit to do the liturgy—for the term *liturgy* means *common action* or *common work*—the Church becomes what it is and expresses its being and life among men.

There is no other manifestation of the Church on earth as the Church of God except in and through the liturgical assembly. It is here that all the faithful are gathered and the Scriptures come alive. It is here that the reality of man's communion with God and each other and all of creation, in truth and in love—the "reality" defended by the Church's dogmas and witnessed by the saints—is realized and experienced by those who are being saved. Everything which is truly in and of the Church is manifested and made available to the faithful in the sacramental, liturgical gathering of the mystical Body with Christ its Head, in the Spirit of God.

A person formally enters the Church by baptism through which he or she dies to this world, with and in Christ, and arises with him into "newness of life"—the eternal life of the Kingdom of God. Baptism is a human being's personal Easter, a "passover" from death to life in the Messiah.

Do you not know that all of us who have been baptized into Christ Jesus were baptized into his death? We were buried therefore with him by baptism into death, so that as Christ was raised from the dead by the glory of the Father, we too might walk in newness of life. For if we have been united with him in a death like his, we shall certainly be united with him in a resurrection like his. We know that our old self was crucified with him so that the sinful body might be destroyed, and we might no longer be enslaved to sin. For he who has died is freed from sin. But if we have died with Christ, we believe that we shall also live with him. For we knew that Christ being raised from the dead will never die again; death no longer has dominion over him. The death he died he died to sin, once for all, but the life he lives he lives to God. So you also must consider yourselves dead to sin and alive to God in Christ Jesus. [Romans 6:3-11]

Baptism, therefore, is not primarily a ritual of washing. It is certainly not the "washing away of the guilt of the original sin." According to the Eastern Church fathers, there is no such thing as the "guilt" of the original sin, and the baptismal liturgy of the Orthodox Church makes no reference to such a thing. Rather, humankind is bound by corruption and death in a sin-filled world which is enslaved by the power of evil. Humankind must be delivered from this corrupted, mortal, and demonic situation. Deliverance comes in Christ, in his incarnation, death, and resurrection. In him, we are redeemed, saved, and liberated from all that captivates and enslaves us. In him, we die and are "born again of water and the Spirit" in order to "enter the Kingdom of God" where there is no sin, no suffering, no death, but life everlasting. (Cf. John 3:5-8) Baptism is primarily death and resurrection in Christ into God's "new creation" (Galatians 6:15) by the power of the Spirit of God.

Wherefore, O King who lovest mankind, come now and sanctify this water by the indwelling of Thy Holy Spirit.

And grant unto it the grace of redemption, the blessing of Jordan. Make it a fountain of incorruption, the gift of sanctification, the remission of sins, the remedy of infirmities, the final destruction of demons, unassailable by hostile powers, filled with angelic might.

But do Thou, O Master, show this water to be the water of sanctification, the purification of flesh and spirit, the loosing of bonds, the remission of sins, the illumination of the soul, the laver of regeneration, the gift of divine sonship, the garment of incorruption, the fountain of life.

For Thou O Lord has said: Wash ye, be ye clean; put away evil things from your souls. Thou hast bestowed upon us a new birth from on high through water and the Holy Spirit.

Wherefore, O Lord, manifest Thyself in this water, and grant that he who is baptized in it may be transformed, that he may put away from himself the old man which is corrupted through the lusts of the flesh, and that he may be clothed with the new man, and renewed after the image of Him who created him; that being buried, after the pattern of Thy death in baptism, he may in like manner be a partaker of Thy resurrection, and having preserved the gift of the Holy Spirit, and increased the measure of grace given to him, he may receive the prize of his high calling and be numbered with the first-born whose names are written in heaven, in Thee our God and Lord Jesus Christ.
[Orthodox Baptismal Liturgy]

After being immersed three times, in the name of the Father and of the Son and of the Holy Spirit, in the consecrated water, which has been called by St. Cyril of Jerusalem the "tomb" and the "womb," the person arises with Christ and is anointed in him with "the seal of the gift of the Holy Spirit." This is the sacrament of chrismation which, in the Eastern tradition, is understood as the person's personal Pentecost.

Called "chrismation" because it is an anointing with "chrism," a consecrated oil, the person is given the gift of the life-creating Spirit of God in order to live the life into which he has been born in baptism. All parts of his body are anointed that the person might indeed be wholly a "christ" through him who is The Christ, that the Spirit of God might descend and remain upon him, enabling him to fulfill in his own way the new humanity of Christ.

As the Spirit comes when the Messiah is glorified; as the Pentecost of the Spirit necessarily follows the Pascha of the Christ; and as life itself necessarily follows birth,—so the sacrament of chrismation, in the Eastern view, necessarily follows baptism and essentially goes together with it. It is for this reason that the practice of "confirmation" long after baptism, and even after the reception of the eucharist, is considered an incorrect practice by the Orthodox Church. For "confirmation" is the sealing of the new-born Christian with the Spirit of God that the person might live. It is not, in the Eastern view, a ritual of personal acceptance and confirmation in the faith by one coming to adulthood.

O Lord God Almighty. . . Who has been graciously pleased to give new birth to Thy servant who has newly received illumination by water and the Spirit. . . . Do Thou the same Master, compassionate King of Kings, grant also unto him the seal of the gift of Thy holy and almighty and adorable Spirit, and participation in the holy Body and precious Blood of Thy Christ.

Keep him in this sanctification. Confirm him in the Orthodox faith. Deliver him from the evil one, and all his temptations. And preserve his soul in purity and unrightness through the saving fear of Thee that he may please Thee in every word and deed and may be a child and heir of Thy heavenly kingdom.

Lay thine almighty hand upon him and preserve him by the power of thy goodness. Maintain unassailed the earnest of the Holy Spirit, and make him worthy of life everlasting. . . .

Maintain the shield of his faith unassailed by the enemy [i.e. the devil]. Preserve pure and undefiled the garment of incorruption wherewith thou hast endowed him, upholding inviolate in him by Thy grace the seal of the Spirit. . . .

Thou art justified. Thou art illumined. Thou art sanctified. Thou art washed. Thou hast received the anointing with the chrism. In the name of our Lord Jesus Christ and by the Spirit of our God. [*Orthodox Chrismation Liturgy; cf. 1 Corinthians 6:11*]

What is given in chrismation is not merely the gifts of the Spirit, the "charismata," but the Spirit himself as gift, the Spirit who comes himself, in his own person, to unite himself with our persons, becoming "one Spirit" with us, thereby making us "christs," the anointed children of God, "one Spirit" with the Father.

But it is God who establishes us with you in Christ, and has commissioned us; he has put his seal upon us and has given us his Spirit in our hearts as a guarantee. [*2 Corinthians 1:21-22*]

In him you also, who have heard the word of truth, the gospel of your salvation, and have believed in him, were sealed with the promised Holy Spirit, which is the guarantee of our inheritance until we acquire possession of it, to the praise of his glory. [*Ephesians 1:13-14*]

Having become worthy of this holy chrism, you are called Christians, making the name truly yours by the new birth [*of baptism*]. *Before you were worthy of this grace, you did not truly deserve this name, but you were on the way. . . .*

It is necessary that you should know that the figure is to be found in the Old Testament. . . but to you, not in figure but in Truth, since you have been really anointed with the Holy Spirit. For the source of your salvation is the Anointed One [*Christ*].

Baptized in Christ, and having put on Christ [*Galatians 3:27*], *you have been conformed to the Son of God. God. . . . has conformed you to the body of the glory of Christ. Becoming participants in Christ, you are rightly called Christ.*

But you were made christs when you received the sacrament of the

Holy Spirit [i.e. chrismation]. And all things were done symbolically because you are images of Christ.

. . .you received the anointing, the sacrament of that with which Christ Himself was anointed, I mean to say, the Holy Spirit, of whom the blessed Isaiah spoke, speaking in the name of the Lord when he said: "The Spirit of the Lord is upon me, for He has anointed me." [Isaiah 61:1-2, Luke 4:18; St. Cyril of Jerusalem, Catechetical Orations)

This same teaching can be found in the writings of Cyprian in Carthage, Gregory in Cappadocia, Ambrose in Milan, and John Chrysostom in Syria. It is a universal doctrine of the Catholic Church.

Following baptism and chrismation, the newly-born, newly-sealed Christian and temple of the Spirit participates in the holy eucharist, the very sacrament of the Church's being and life as the Kingdom of God on earth; what St. Maximus the Confessor has called the "mystery of mysteries."

In the Eastern Church, even small children who are baptized into Christ and sealed with God's Spirit are brought to the eucharistic table to participate in the mystical supper of the Lord, the "marriage supper of the Lamb" in the Kingdom of God. (Cf. Revelation 19:9) This practice is defended on the belief that human persons can be sanctified by God from infancy to grow and develop "in wisdom and in stature, and in favor before God and man," as did Jesus himself, with the new, eternal, and abundant life of God's Kingdom in Christ and the Spirit. (Cf. Luke 2:52) It is also defended on the belief that there is no "moment" when one consciously joins the Church through an adult act of faith (certainly not an act made in the early teens), but that the "act of faith" through which one affirms allegiance to Christ—and thereby accepts his or her membership in the Church—must be done in every moment of one's life, by the *acts* of one's life, reborn and reconfirmed by continual participation each Lord's day in the holy eucharist. When one cannot and does not make such an act of faith by a continual dying and rising in Christ through a perpetual reception of the gift of God's Spirit, then one is out of the Church in fact, and participates in the eucharistic life of the Church, if at all, "in an unworthy manner," and is "guilty of profaning the body and blood of the Lord" and, therefore, "eats and drinks judgment upon himself" (Cf. 1 Corinthians 11:27-29) Thus, in the Orthodox view, as a person grows, he or she accepts or rejects faith in God, and his baptism and chrismation, by his continual deeds, and not by any "once and for all" affirmation accomplished in words. And the sign of this affirmation is the faithful participation in the Lord's day eucharist in a worthy manner, "discerning the Lord's Body" in humble and perpetually repentant love and devotion.

Participation in the mystery of the eucharist is participation in Christ's eternal self-offering to the Father in the Spirit, which is the very life of the Church. Human persons participate in this life by the "grace of the Lord Jesus Christ and the love of God and the fellowship of the Holy Spirit." (2 Corinthians 13:14) The eucharist itself, like the life of the Church, is the "communion of the Holy Spirit," communion with God, who is love, through the grace of Christ. The prayers of the eucharistic liturgy of St. John Chrysostom confirm this again and again throughout the sacramental action.

O Lord God Almighty. . .make us worthy to find grace in Thy sight, that our sacrifice may be acceptable to Thee and that the Good Spirit of Thy grace may dwell upon us, and upon these gifts here offered, and upon all Thy people. [Offertory Prayer]

After the *anaphora,* when all praise and thanksgiving is offered to God and to his only-begotten Son and his Holy Spirit, when the saving events of the Messiah are recalled over the gifts of bread and wine, and when the gifts are lifted up to God the Father "in behalf of all and for all," the prayer continues:

Send down Thy Holy Spirit upon us and upon these gifts here offered.

And make this bread the most precious Body of Thy Christ.

And that which is in this cup the most precious Blood of Thy Christ.

Changing them by Thy Holy Spirit.

In the Russian Orthodox tradition, the "prayer of the third hour" is also recited at this point in the liturgy.

O Lord Who at the third hour didst send down Thy Holy Spirit upon thine apostles, take not the same Spirit from us, O Good One, but renew Him in us who make our supplications to Thee.

Create in me a clean heart O God and put a new and right Spirit within me.

Cast me not away from Thy presence and take not Thy Holy Spirit from me.

And then, after the consecration, the liturgical prayer goes on:

That these gifts may be for those who partake for the purification of soul, for the remission of sins, for the communion of the Holy Spirit, for the fulfillment of the Kingdom of heaven. . . .

And then again, after the "remembrances" and before the Lord's Prayer:

Make us worthy, O Master, Who lovest mankind, to partake of the heavenly and awesome mysteries of this sacred and spiritual table with a pure conscience, for the remission of sins, for the forgiveness of transgressions, for the communion of the Holy Spirit, for the inheritance of the Kingdom of heaven. . .

And then again after Holy Communion, all the faithful sing:

We have seen the True Light!
We have received the heavenly Spirit!
We have found the True Faith!

Worshipping the Undivided Trinity, Who has saved us!

Just as the eucharistic liturgy is offered by Christ, and it is Christ who is offered and received, so the liturgy is accomplished by the Holy Spirit and the "communion of the Holy Spirit" is its result. This is the character of the liturgy, as it is the character of life itself. Christ is in us by the power of the Spirit, enabling us, by the power of the same Spirit, to be in him—and so to be in communion with God his Father as our own Father, in the Spirit.

According to the Orthodox faith, the *epiklesis*, the "calling forth" of the Holy Spirit on the faithful as well as on the gifts of bread and wine, is an essential element in the eucharistic action. It cannot be overlooked, or merely "mentioned in passing." It is a central act, affirming the fact that only in and by the Spirit of God does the Church live and act. For Christ himself has accomplished his self-offering to the Father through the Holy Spirit, who is in him and on him as the anointed of God.

For if the sprinkling of defiled persons with the blood of goats and bulls and with the ashes of a heifer sanctifies for the purification of the flesh, how much more shall the blood of Christ, who through the eternal Spirit offered himself without blemish to God, purify your conscience from dead works to serve the living God. [Hebrews 9:13-14]

Thus, the Church also offers itself to God in Christ its high priest "through the Eternal Spirit," and this must be explicitly enacted in the liturgical action of the eucharist, for without it, the offering cannot be made, and the faithful, with their gifts, cannot be sanctified. The Holy Spirit enables all things in the life of man and most primarily his communion with God through Christ in the Church.

All things are accomplished in humankind by God through Christ in the Spirit. Even when a person sins, repentance is enabled and effected by the Holy Spirit in the Church. The sacrament of reconciliation, accomplished by heartfelt confession and the reaffirmation of baptismal promises, is possible because of the

Lord's gift of the Spirit in the Church to forgive and retain the sins of men and women. (Cf. John 20:21-22)

O Lord God, the salvation of Thy servants, gracious, bountiful and long-suffering. . . grant unto Thy servant the image of repentance, forgiveness of sins and deliverance, pardoning every transgression, voluntary and involuntary. Reconcile and unite him to Thy Holy Church, through Jesus Christ our Lord. . . .[Liturgy of Confession]

Because one is baptized and chrismated, one's sins can be forgiven within the community of grace if repentance is real and a return to the Father is accomplished with the genuine desire to be reconciled and united to his Holy Church, by the grace of the Savior who remains eternally in the Church as the reconciling mediator between God and humankind, by the power of his Holy Spirit.

In the Church as well, the love of man and woman can be sanctified by God's Spirit to participate forever in the Kingdom of God. The sacrament of marriage in the Orthodox Church, is not a "legal contract" sworn by a man and woman to remain together until parted in death. Rather, it is the offering of the couple's unity in love to God in Christ so that this loving union might be made perfect by God's Spirit of love and be fulfilled in the Kingdom of God.

In the Orthodox liturgy of marriage, there are no vows ("oaths" of any kind are not allowed in the Orthodox Church because of Christ's specific commandment forbidding them, cf. Matthew 5:33-37). And in the Orthodox ceremony, there is no mention of "parting in death," since the whole point of the sacrament is that there should be and can be no "parting" of any kind in Christ and the Church.

For I am sure that neither death, nor life, nor angels, nor principalities, nor things present, nor things to come, nor powers, nor height, nor depth, nor anything else in all creation, will be able to separate us from the love of God in Christ Jesus our Lord. [Romans 8:38-39]

The Orthodox liturgy of marriage is consciously patterned after the liturgy of baptism and the eucharist. The couple come to the Church already united as far as "this world" is concerned. They come to offer their human unity of love to God in Christ. They come to ask that they may die together to "this world" and be alive together in Christ forever in God's Kingdom. They come that the Holy Spirit may descend upon them and make their love to be the image of the perfect, eternally faithful love of God for the world, of the Lord for Israel, and of Christ for the Church. They come that "united in one mind" and "wedded into one flesh," they may be united in the one "mind" and the one "flesh" of Christ himself, in the communion of his one Holy Spirit in God forever.

According to the Scriptures, the relationship between God and his creatures is a relationship of conjugal love. It is a love to which God is faithful in every condition, no matter now adulterous is his bride. (cf. Isaiah 54:5, Jeremiah 3:32, Hosea) It is this love, perfectly shown in the love of Christ the Bridegroom for the Church his Bride (Matthew 9:15, John 3:29, Revelation 21:9), that is to be realized and fulfilled in marriage in the Church. For this reason, the gospel reading at the marriage liturgy is not Christ's rigorous teaching about divorce but the account of the wedding feast in Cana of Galilee, where Jesus shows forth his first messianic sign by granting the transformation of water into good wine. And it is for this reason as well that the wedding epistle reading is from the Letter to the Ephesians.

. . .always and for everything giving thanks in the name of our Lord Jesus Christ to God the Father.

Be subject to one another out of reverence for Christ. Wives, be subject to your husbands, as to the Lord. For the husband is the head of the wife as Christ is the head of the church, his body, and is himself its Savior. As the church is subject to Christ, so let wives also be subject in everything to their husbands. Husbands, love your wives, as Christ loved the church and gave himself up for her, that he might sanctify her, having cleansed her by the washing of water with the word, that he might present the church to himself in splendor, without spot or wrinkle or any such thing, that she might be holy

and without blemish. Even so husbands should love their
wives as their own bodies. He who loves his wife loves himself. For
no man ever hates his own flesh, but nourishes and cherishes it, as
Christ does the church, because we are members of his body. "For
this reason a man shall leave his father and mother and be joined to
his wife, and the two shall become one flesh." This is a great
mystery, and I take it to mean Christ and the church; however, let
each one of you love his wife as himself, and let the wife see that she
respects her husband. [*Ephesians 5:20-33*]

This biblical view of marriage is not popular today. It is rejected
even by many who call themselves Christians. It is rejected not
simply because of the supposedly demeaning and degrading position
it gives to the wife, but also because of the self-emptying,
self-sacrificing, and self-crucifying love that it requires of the
husband. The problem here is not simply one of "women's
liberation." It is the problem of "man's liberation" as well, at least
from the traditional Christian point of view.

The problem today, indeed the crime and the sin, is that "fallen
man," the "old Adam," is the norm of value and success in our
world. If this were the case simply for "this world," the problem
would be slight, for it would be normal. But the image of fallen man,
the fallen "male," has become accepted as natural and normative
even by Christians. And theologies and lifestyles are built on this
foolishness.

Any sort of "submission" or "subjection"—even to one another
in the Lord, to one another "out of reverence for Christ"—is considered unworthy and degrading. People are not to be submitted
or subjected to one another for any reason; and even submission or
subjection to God is considered beneath human dignity as a form of
tyranny and enslavement. Yet, according to the scriptures, Christ
himself is submitted and subjected in all things to God his Father;
speaking the Father's words, doing the Father's work, and
accomplishing the Father's will. Christ claims to have nothing but
what he has received from God, and is totally obedient to him in
everything "even unto death, death on the cross." (Philippians 2:8)
And even then, when "God has highly exalted him and bestowed on

him the name that is above every name" (Philippians 2:9), even then
he subjects himself to the Father for eternity, and this is considered to
be his glory and perfection.

Although he was a Son, he learned obedience through what he
suffered; and being made perfect he became the source of salvation
to all who obey him. . . .[Hebrews 5:8-9]

"For God has put all things in subjection under his feet." But when it
says, "All things are put in subjection under him," it is plain that he
is excepted who put all things under him, then the Son himself will
also be subjected to him who put all things under him, that God may
be all in all. [1 Corinthians 15:27-28]

To be subject to God in all things and obedient to him onto death
is the glory of Christ. (Cf. John 13:31). It is his exaltation and
dignity, his majesty and honor, the sign of his power, divinity, and
equality with God. It is the proof that the Father is "greater" than he
is. (John 14:28). And yet that he is "in the Father" and the Father is
"in him" (John 14:11) and that he and the Father "are one" (John
10:30). This is the Christian vision of man, and man with God, man
deified and glorified with all the fulness of divine being and life. It is
this that we come to know in the Spirit of God, the "Spirit of truth,"
whom the world cannot receive, because it "neither sees him nor
knows him. . .," (John 14:17).

For all that is in the world; the lust of the flesh and the lust of the eyes
and the pride of life, is not of the Father but is of the world. And the
world passes away, and the lust of it; but he who does the will of
God abides forever. [1 John 2:16-17]

Success in society today is the success of the old Adam,
the fallen male. It is the success of the "lust of the flesh" and the
"pride of life." When such a vision of success becomes the normative
realization of perfect dignity, freedom, and equality, there is no
reason at all why women should not be as "successful" as men, with a
full share of the action and an "equal opportunity" to partake of the

fruits of such "achievement." How otherwise can it be understood to be a cause of rejoicing when "women too" can demonstrate "success" and "achievement" by wielding power, gaining profit, and attaining prestige in this world with a full share in the "pride of life"?

No, the problem is not "women's liberation," as if men were already liberated. The problem is "human liberation"—human liberation from the view that subjection, humility, and obedience are demeaning and degrading from the view that to be a "head" is to be a tyrant and to be "submissive" is to be a slave, from the conviction that to love is to lust, and to lead is to wield prideful power. It is human liberation from the idea that in the human community, especially the community of marriage, the model of Christ and the Church must be rejected and destroyed as if God himself in Christ has "raped" his creation and enslaved it to himself as a tyrannous, prideful, and lustful male. In fact, Christ has loved his creation in humble dignity and majestic respect for the one whom he has made to be his Body and his Bride, in perfect freedom and with her full cooperation.

On this point, the words of St. John Chrysostom written in the fourth century, remain unparalled in Christian tradition:

. . .from the beginning God has made special provision for this union; and discoursing on the two as one, He has said, "male and female created He them." [Genesis 1:27] And again, "There is neither male nor female." [Galatians 3:28] For there is no relationship between humans so close as between man and wife, if they be joined together as they should be.

For there is nothing which so welds our life together as the love of man and wife.

. . . "wives be in subjection unto your own husbands, as unto the Lord."

. . . primarily for the Lord's sake. . . as serving the Lord. . . . And

why so? Because when they are in harmony, the children are well
brought up and the household is in good order— for indeed a house
is a small church—and the neighbors and friends and relations enjoy
the fragrance. But if it be otherwise, all is turned upside down and
thrown into confusion.

He had already laid down beforehand for man and wife, the ground
and provision for their love, assigning to each their proper place, to
the one that of authority and forethought, and to the other than of
submission. And then "the church", that is, both husbands and
wives, "is subject to Christ. . . ." [for "the head of Christ is
God."—1 Corinthians 11:3]

You have seen the measure of obedience, hear also the measure of
love, Would you then have a wife obedient unto you, as the Church
is to Christ? Take then yourself the same provident care for her as
Christ takes for the Church. Yea, even if it shall be needful for you to
give your life for her, yea, and to be cut into pieces a thousand times,
yea, and to undergo and endure any suffering whatever—do not
refuse it. Though you should undergo all this, you will not even then
have done anything like Christ! For you indeed are doing this for one
to whom you are already knit; but He for one who turned her back
on Him and hated Him.

A servant, indeed, one perhaps may be able to bind down by
fear. . . .But the partner of one's life, the mother of one's children,
the foundation of one's every joy, one ought never to chain down by
fear and menaces but by love and good temper.

Yes, though you should suffer anything on her account, do not
upbraid her, for neither did Christ do this.

"And He gave Himself up," Paul says, "that He might sanctify and
cleanse. . . ." Whatever kind of wife you shall take, you shall never
take such a bride as the Church when Christ took her, nor one so far
removed from you as the Church was from Christ!

*"This is a great mystery: but I speak of Christ and the Church." Why
does He call it a great mystery? Because it was something great and
wonderful that the blessed Moses, or rather God Himself, intimated.
For the present however, he says, I speak regarding Christ, that
having left the Father, He came down and joined Himself to the Bride
and became One Spirit [with her] as it is written: "For he who is
joined to the Lord is one Spirit with Him." [1 Corinthians 6:17]
The wife is a second authority [as the Spirit is the second Advocate];
let her not then demand equality for she is under the head; nor let
him despise her as being in subjection, for she is the body; and if the
head despise the body, it will itself perish. But let him bring in love
on his part. . . . [and] provide for the body, seeing it contains every
sense in itself. Nothing can be better than this union!*

*This then is marriage when it takes place according to Christ,
spiritual marriage and spiritual birth. . . Yea a marriage it is, not of
passion, nor of flesh, but wholly spiritual, the soul being united to
God by a union unspeakable and which He alone knows. Therefore
he says, "He that is joined to the Lord is one Spirit with Him." Mark
how earnestly he endeavors to unite both flesh with flesh and spirit
with spirit. [Homily 20—on Ephesians]*

I refer to these words of St. John Chrysostom, which may appear
outdated, romantic, and naive, not so much to demonstrate the
place of the woman in marriage as to show what, according to the
saints, is the place of the man and the ideal of life for those who are
Christians. For the real problem, I repeat, is that of the meaning of all
human life. It is, most concretely, the question of what is considered
as success and achievement for those in the Church who have
become one Spirit with God in Christ.

Concerning the image of the "great mystery" of Christ and the
Church, there is more to be said about the union in marriage.
According to the catholic tradition, the Church itself is the Bride of
Christ because it is filled with God's Spirit. The Church is "full of
grace" because the Spirit of God fills the Church with his divine
presence, hiding himself (the expression is that of Vladimir Lossky)
behind the person of Christ and the multitude of persons who form
his body and his bride. It is in this sense that the Church is a

"she"—as Mother and Bride—and the "icon" of the Church is the holy Virgin Mary, the mother of Christ, who symbolizes the entire company of the saved, united in love with the Lord. Thus, it might be said that as the Word and the Spirit are in perfect unity and harmony with the Father in the divine Holy Trinity, and as the Word and the Spirit are in perfect unity and harmony in the creation and salvation of the world by God, and as Christ the Head is in perfect unity and harmony with his Spirit-filled Body and Bride comprising God's Church, so the husband and wife are to be in perfect unity and harmony in the divine union of marriage.

Following this imagery, no one can dare to say that in the divine Holy Trinity, or in the dispensation of creation and salvation, or in the life of the Church, the Holy Spirit is "demeaned" or "degraded" by his interrelation with Christ, and even his "subordination" to Christ in the perfect unity and harmony of divine being and action. The Holy Spirit is as divine and as perfect as the Father and the Son, with exactly the same divine nature. There is no inequality among the persons of the Trinity. And yet, in the perfect interpersonal relationship within the Godhead itself—the perfect interrelationship of divine being and life, of divine love itself—there is a sense in which the Holy Spirit lives and acts for the glory of Christ, and for the glory of those who are "made christs" through him by the Spirit's own actions.

The point to be seen here is this: If one accepts with utter seriousness the fact that the Godhead is a Trinity of equal divine persons, and if one believes that within the Divine Trinity there is an "order" of interpersonal relations, and if one believes as well that in God's relations with his creatures he acts as he does through Christ and the Holy Spirit, one will understand that the relationship between men and women in marriage is a pattern of Divine Love in which there is nothing degrading and demeaning to the one whose action in marriage is compared to that of the Spirit-filled Church in her unity with Christ.

I believe that God created human beings according to his own image and likeness because of the trinitarian character of the Divine Nature, and that the proper interrelationship between the sexes within the order of creation is patterned after the interrelationship between God's Son and his Spirit. This divine interrelationship is the "prototype" of the union of love between a man and a woman in the community of marriage. I would only offer on this point, admittedly undeveloped in Christian theology, the fact that the holy fathers, particularly Saint Gregory the Theologian, insist that the Godhead is not merely a "unity" but a "union." Within this "union" there is a definite "order" of relationships, which is perfectly divine, yet which includes a distinction of personal "modes of existence" in which the Son and the Spirit have a definite form of relationship, manifested to the world in the revelation of God through Christ and the Spirit in the dispensation of salvation, which is perfectly fulfilled and realized in the life of the Church. For, Christ is the King and the Spirit is the Kingship. Christ is the Anointed and the Spirit is the Unction. Christ is the Head and the Spirit fills his Body. Christ is the Bridegroom, and the Spirit dwells in his Bride. And Christ and the Spirit are perfectly one in their inseparable unity in God, who is love.

Halleujah! For the Lord our God the Almighty reigns.
Let us rejoice and exult and give him glory.
For the marriage of the Lamb has come,
and His Bride has made herself ready. . . .

"Behold I am coming soon. . .
I am the Alpha and the Omega. . . .
I Jesus. . . I am the root and the offspring of David. . . ."

And the Spirit and the Bride say, "Come!"
And let him who hears say, "Come."

Surely I am coming soon. Amen. Come Lord Jesus!
                    [Revelation 19:6-7, 22:12,17,20]

Those who can utter these words in faith are those who are blessed to be "invited to the marriage supper of the Lamb." (Revelation 19:9) They are also those who know that human marriage has meaning only as the image and likeness of this divine marriage—the great mystery of Christ and Church—prefigured in conjugal love from the beginning and fulfilled forever in the Kingdom of God. It is for this reason that the sacramental ritual of marriage in the Eastern Church is a "crowning" for life everlasting with God.

Blessed art Thou, O Lord our God, the Priest of mystical and pure marriage, the Lawgiver of the marriage of the body, the Preserver of incorruption and the Provider of earthly blessings. . . . Do Thou now, O Master, Who in the beginning didst make man and set him to be as it were King over creation and didst say: It is not good for man to be alone on the earth. . . .

O Lord our God, crown them with glory and honor! Thou hast set upon their heads crowns of precious stones; they asked life of Thee, and Thou gavest it them. For thou wilt give them Thy blessings forever and ever; Thou wilt make them to rejoice with gladness through Thy presence.

Cause their marriage to be honorable. Preserve their bed blameless. Mercifully grant that they may live together in purity. . .walking in Thy commandments with a pure heart. . . . Receive their crowns into Thy Kingdom, preserving them stainless, blameless and without shame for ages and ages. [*Orthodox Marriage Liturgy*]

Man's way into God's Kingdom necessarily passes through death. The "martyr's crown" belongs to those who bear witness to Christ's victory of life (the word *martyr* means *witness*) through their own suffering and death in the flesh together with him.

If we have died with him, we shall also live with him;
If we endure, we shall also reign with him [*2 Timothy 2:11-12*]

The sacrament of Holy Unction in the Church is the consecration of human suffering by the Spirit of God, so that human suffering can be a living testimony to the power of Christ, so that human death can be itself an act of life.

The normal way in which people deal with suffering and death, in our time, is to avoid suffering at all costs, and then to accept it when, inevitably, it comes, facing it courageously and with stoic resignation or to deny it and curse it to the end. But in the Christian view, resignation is not the final word—and still less is it murder, mercifully inflicted, either by one's own hand or through the benevolence of others. The final word of the Christian in the face of suffering is to transform the suffering itself into an act of affirmation and life, and to use it as the means of attaining Christlike perfection.

For it was fitting that he, for whom and by whom all things exist, in bringing many sons to glory, should make the pioneer of their salvation perfect through suffering. [Hebrews 2:10]

Now I rejoice in my sufferings. . . and in my flesh I complete what is lacking in Christ's afflictions for the sake of the body, that is the Church. . . . [Colossians 1:24]

In the Christian view, suffering must be overcome by its inner transformation, by its inner consecration by God's Spirit into the powerful means of defeating the devil and conquering death. The sacrament of holy unction exists for this purpose. It is not merely the form of "last rites" before immediate death—a kind of final insurance against the fires of hell. Neither is it a last attempt to coerce a miracle of healing from the hands of God when all other means have failed. It is rather the sacrament and prayer which invokes the real miracle and the real victory of life over death, the victorious miracle and the miraculous victory of a person making his "passion" a voluntary self-offering of faith in God, the living witness to God's healing power of love in man: the power "made perfect in weakness." (2 Corinthians 12:9)

The Church rejoices in Thee, O Christ, crying aloud:
Thou art my fortress, O Lord, my refuge and my strength.

The Church, beholding Thee uplifted on the Cross, O Son of Righteousness, stands in its dignity, worthily crying aloud: Glory to Thy power, O Lord.

O Saviour, Who like chrism incorruptible dost empty Thyself utterly in grace to purify the world: show mercy and bounty, in godlike manner, upon the bodily wounds of Thy servant who, with faith, is to receive holy unction.

Through the anointing with thine oil and the touch of thy priests, O Lover of Man, sanctify thy servant from on high. Free him from his infirmities. Purge away his spiritual illness. Wash him, O Saviour, and deliver him from greatly alluring temptations. Assuage his maladies. Banish all obstacles. Utterly destroy all his afflictions, forasmuch as Thou art bountiful and full of loving-kindness.

Let us pray. . . that the Lord will bless this oil by the power and action and descent of the Holy Spirit. . . .

For the servant of God, and for his visitation in God, that the grace of the Holy spirit may come upon him. . . .

. . . that putting away earthly lusts, we may die unto sin, and live unto righteousness, being clothed upon Him through the anointing with sanctification of the oil. . . .

Let this oil, O Lord, become the oil of gladness, the oil of sanctification, a royal robe, an armor of light, the averting of every work of the devil, the seal of immunity from snares, the joy of the heart, an eternal rejoicing, that he who is anointed with this oil of regeneration may be fearful to his adversaries, and may shine in the radiance of Thy saints, having no spot or wrinkle, and may attain unto everlasting rest and receive the prize of his high calling. . . .
[*Orthodox Liturgy of Holy Unction*]

Once again we have the radical transformation of that which, according to the "old Adam," is death and defeat, unto that which in Christ is victory and life. And this comes by the Spirit of God.

The guarantee of the Spirit's presence in the Church, making Christ himself present and active in all the fulness of his divine, messianic presence and power, is the sacrament of the priesthood. In the Orthodox view, the pastoral office in the Church is a *mysterion*, a sacrament belonging essentially and necessarily to the being and life of the Church. The pastoral office in the Church is not a human invention, nor a practical necessity required in the Church as a human institution. Neither is it a personal or private charism," given to individuals for their own salvation or for some specific purpose of edification. It is a gift of God to his people in the Church, guaranteeing Christ's presence and power among men—the "life of the Holy Spirit in humanity." It is the gift of God, insuring the identity and continuity of his Church as "the fulness of him who fills all in all" in all times and places: teaching, guiding, healing, forgiving, reconciling, sanctifying, saving.

Because the sacrament of the pastoral office is of the very essence of the Church, in and for the Church, it has no meaning when taken by itself outside the being and life of the covenant community. The priestly sacrament, as the sacrament of Christ's presence in the Church, is always exercised within the body, together with the body, as an essential element of the entire doctrinal, spiritual, and sacramental life of the body. This is so simply because the body is never without its head, as the bride is never without her bridegroom. The priesthood is not a "vicarious representation" of Christ who is "in heaven." It is not God's gift of power to men to exercise Christ's prerogatives in his absence. Christ is forever in the Church, bringing "all the fulness of God" to men in the Holy Spirit, "always, even unto the end of the ages." (Matthew 28:20)

With this understanding of the priesthood as the sacrament of the "presentation" (and not "representation") of Christ in the Church as the Head and the Bridegroom, it is equally understood by the Orthodox that the proper bearer and expressor of this mystery—its "living image"—must be a male member of the Church, and not a female member. This does not mean that males are "better Christians" than females, as it does not mean that priests are "better Christians" than lay persons. In fact, if the priesthood were merely the "image" and "manifestation" of the "good Christian," it would most suitably be imaged and signified sacramentally by a female, according to traditional biblical and spiritual "symbolics," since the "best Christian" and the image and manifestation of the Church as the Body and Bride of Christ is Mary, the Theotokos, and not Christ, the incarnate Logos.

It is pertinent here that the icon of the Virgin Mary in the attitude of prayer, with Christ within her, traditionally placed over the altar area in Eastern Christian church buildings, is not an icon of Mary as such. It is called the icon of *The Sign*: "For the Lord Himself will give you this sign. Behold, a virgin shall conceive and bear a son and shall call his name Immanuel, which means, God with us " (Isaiah 7:14) This is the Church: God with us through Christ and the Holy Spirit, who comes to human persons making them "full of grace," the "dwelling place of God in the Spirit," by forming Christ in them.

Thus the priesthood, sacramentally and liturgically, is the sign of Christ in the Church, the Head and the Bridegroom. It is not the sign of the "members of Christ," his body and his bride. It is the sign of the one Good Pastor and the one Great High Priest, and not the sign of the Shepherd's sheep or the High Priest's subjects. It is the sign of the Logos enfleshed, and not the sign of his Spirit-filled temple. If one does not believe or accept this view of the priesthood, if one rather thinks that the priesthood is no sacrament at all, or merely the consecration and ordination of the "best Christian" exercising power and authority on and over others in the body as one of the members enabled and entrusted to do this—whether by God, or by the body, or by both in some fashion, because of some particular gifts such as "leadership ability" or "administrative prowess" or "eloquence of speech" or "theological acumen"—then, of course, it is reasonable to believe that any member of the Church whatever his or her sex, can do this equally well, since indeed it is true that in Christ "there is neither male nor female. . . for as many as have been baptized into Christ have put on Christ. . .and you are all one in Christ." (Galatians 3:27-28)

But it is precisely the belief of the Orthodox, and the entire catholic tradition of the Church until today, that the priestly and pastoral office in the Church is *not* the image of the saved, but of the Savior; of Christ himself as Head, Bridegroom, Good Shepherd, and High Priest; of Christ, and so of God himself, acting toward his creatures in the movement of revelation, creation, and salvation in love. The priestly office is not an individual gift or a personal charisma. And so, the Church teaches that the proper realization of this sacrament in the Church is not possible through every member of the Church. It excludes, as St. John Chrysostom has said, not only "all women"—including the Theotokos herself—but "most men" as well. (*On the Priesthood*) And once more, let us stress it, this is because the nature of the priestly sacrament requires its expression in the body through the male image, by a male form, in a male action, because the man who fulfills this sacrament has no other purpose than to present the image, and to image the presence, of Christ in the body. He is not the "best member" or the "expert Christian". He is not the efficient administrator or the charismatic holy man, the eloquent orator or the practitioner of prophetic gifts. He is not the psychological counsellor or the accomplished social organizer, the academic scholar or the intellectual theologian. And, he is certainly not the sacerdotal potentate. He is expressly the one who, in and for the body, manifests Christ in all the power of His messianic presence; the one who, without any other particular or specific qualification, presides in "the place of God." (St. Ignatius of Antioch, 2nd c. *To Magnesians*]

The grace divine, which always heals the infirm and completes that which is wanting, elevated through the laying on of hands the most devout deacon . . . to be a priest. Wherefore, let us pray for him, that the grace of the Holy Spirit might come upon him.

O God, great in might and inscrutable in wisdom, marvelous in counsel above the sins of men: Do Thou, the same Lord, fill with the gift of Thy Holy Spirit this man whom it hath pleased thee to advance to the office of presbyter, that he may stand in innocency before Thine altar; to proclaim the gospel of Thy kingdom; to minister the word of Thy Truth; to offer unto Thee spiritual gifts and sacrifices, to renew thy people through the lover of regeneration. . . . [Orthodox Ordination to the Priesthood]

Do Thou the same Lord, make this man. . . who hath been proclaimed a steward of Thine episcopal grace, to be an imitater of Thee, the true Sheperd, Who didst lay down Thy life for Thy sheep; to be a leader of the blind, a light to those who are in darkness, a reprover of the universe, a teacher of the young, a lamp to the world that. . . he may stand without shame before Thy throne. . . . [Orthodox Consecration to the Episcopate]

Thus it is that the Church of Christ lives by the Spirit of God. Nothing in the Church can be done without him. For it is indeed as the Orthodox Church sings on the great feast of Pentecost:

The Holy Spirit provides all things.
He overflows with prophecy.
He fulfills the priesthood.
He teaches wisdom to the simple.
He reveals fishermen as theologians.
He gathers together all the laws of the Church.
Equal with the Father in being and power, O Comforter,
Glory to Thee! [*Vespers Hymn of Pentecost*]

CHAPTER V.

THE SPIRIT
IN HUMAN PERSONS

According to the Scriptures and the tradition of the Church, man is the "dwelling place of God in the Spirit" when he fulfills the calling not to be "conformed to this world, but(to) be transformed by the renewal of your mind, that you may prove what is the will of God, what is good and acceptable and perfect." (Romans 12:2) To be the "dwelling place of God in the Spirit" means, in a word, to be "conformed to the image of (God's) Son." (Romans 8:29) This "conforming" to Christ is first of all a transformation and renewal of one's *mind*. It is a "repentance," which literally means a "change of mind"—*metanoia*. To have the Spirit of God is to have the "mind of the Spirit," which is the "mind of Christ." (Romans 8:27, 1 Corinthians 2:16)

In a real sense, therefore, the indwelling of God's Spirit in man is first of all a reversal and renewal of human understanding. It is a new outlook, a new insight into reality. It is, we might say, a vision of things from God's point of view. It is what St. Isaac the Syrian has called a "spiritual gnosis," the "knowledge of hidden realities," the "knowledge of everlasting life." (Cf. *Spiritual Homilies*) Or, to refer to St. Simeon the New Theologian, it is being enlightened and illumined by the light of God himself.

*We do not speak about that of which we are ignorant, but we bear
witness to that which we know. For the light already shines in the
darkness, in the night and in the day, in our minds and hearts. Those
who have not received this light, have not yet received grace, for in
receiving grace [i.e. the Spirit of God] one receives the divine light
and God Himself. Kings or patriarchs, bishops or priests, princes or
slaves, seculars or monastics, all are equally in the shadows and
walk in darkness unless they are willing to repent as they ought to
do. For repentance [metanoia—the transformation of the mind] is
the gate which leads from the realm of darkness into that of light.
Those therefore who are not yet in the light have not yet truly
crossed the threshold of repentance. . . .[1]*

The mysteries of baptism and chrismation, with the entrance into
the eucharistic mystery of the Church, is traditionally called "holy
illumination" in the Eastern Church. This is the way it is referred to
in the liturgical texts and the writing of the Church fathers.

*Illumination [i.e. baptism-chrismation-eucharist] is the splendor of
souls, a conversion of the life, an appeal to God for a clear
conscience. [Cf. 1 Peter 3:21]*

*It is the aid to our weakness, the renunciation of the flesh, the
following of the Spirit, the communion of the Word [i.e. Christ], the
improvement of the creature, the overwhelming of sin, the
participation in the Light, the dissolution of darkness.*

*It is the carriage to God, the dying with Christ, the perfecting of the
mind, the bulwark of faith, the key of the kingdom of God, the
change of life, the removal of slavery, the loosing of chains, the
remodeling of the whole person*

*Why should I go into greater detail? Illumination is the greatest and
most magnificent of the gifts of God. For just as we speak of the Holy*

1.Homily 79, quoted from V. Lossky, *The Mystical Theology of
the Eastern Church,* p. 218-219.

of Holies and the Song of Songs, as more comprehensive and more excellent than others, so is this called Illumination as being more holy that any other illumination which we possess. [St. Gregory the Theologian,.Oration on Holy Baptism]

Did you see how a new creation has truly taken place [through the illumination of baptism]? The grace of God has entered these souls and molded them anew, reformed them, and made them different from what they were [literally, "one person in place of another."] It did not change their essence, but remade their will, no longer permitting the judgment of the mind's eye to entertain an erroneous notion, but by dissipating the fog which was blinding their eyes, God's grace made them all the ugly deformity of evil and the shining beauty of virtue as they really are. [St. John Chrysostom, Baptismal Instructions, IV]

Human wickedness has darkened men's minds. Evil has made the mind, according to the teaching of St. Paul, "base" and "blind," "sensuous" and "senseless." In order for a human being to see things clearly—himself, other persons, the world, and God himself—his spiritual vision must be purified and enlightened. This is done by the indwelling of the Holy Spirit. It is the first and most basic action of the Spirit of God becoming "one Spirit" with man's spirit when he is united to the Lord. (1 Corinthians 6:17) By the grace of the indwelling Spirit, man's mind is purified and his understanding is clarified. He can see reality clearly in the light of God. He can, as St. John has said, "know the truth" and be taught "about everything," because he is "taught by God." This is the main characteristic of the human person in the life of the final and everlasting covenant foretold by the prophets and fulfilled in Christ by the coming of the Holy Spirit. It is the main characteristic of what it means to be filled with the Spirit of God.

When a person is "taught by God," by the Spirit of truth, in the renewal of his mind, the first thing he knows is that he is a sinner. The awareness of sin, primarily one's own sin, is the first insight given to men by God's Spirit of wisdom. It is the certain conviction that man is "missing the mark" in regard to the meaning and purpose of life. It is the absolute conviction that man's life must be recreated and redirected if it will be in conformity with God's son, the divine archetype in whose image and according to whose likeness man is originally made. Thus, to have the Spirit of God in this "sinful and adulterous generation" is not to be sinless, for that is not fully possible for man in this age. It is rather to know what sin is, to know one's own sins and the sins of the world, and to confess them with genuine humility and repentance.

If we say we have no sin, we deceive ourselves, and the truth is not in us. If we confess our sins, he is faithful and just, and will forgive our sins and cleanse us from all unrighteousness. If we say we have not sinned, we make him a liar, and his word is not in us. [1John 1:8-10]

Knowing sin, therefore, and confessing one's own sins and those of the world, with the perfect knowledge that in Christ all "iniquities are forgiven" and all sins are "remembered no more" in the final messianic covenant (Jeremiah 31:34), is the first gift of God's Spirit of wisdom. Only the person filled with the Spirit of God can know this by his own concrete, existential experience. And only such a person can thereby be truly liberated from the sins that enslave him.

This is the paradox of the spiritual life: to know one's sins and to confess them is to be liberated from them. Only the really "holy" know this, and can do it with power and conviction. Only the really holy know with utter certainty "how great is the burden of sin" (the expression of St. Anselm). Certainly, it is not the sinful man who realizes this, caught up as he is in the blindness and baseness of the vain imaginations of his sensuous and senseless mind. To know this gravity, ugliness, and perversity of sin is reserved for the saints. It is the fruit of being in union with God in the Spirit.

Once sin is seen for what it is; once it is exposed, acknowledged, and confessed; more accurately, once it is *continually* and *perpetually* acknowledged and confessed by the grace of God's Spirit in man, the way is clear for genuine human growth and development in the likeness of God. Being made one with God in the Spirit, with true insight into reality, the person can be cleansed "from every defilement of body and spirit and make holiness perfect in the fear of

God." (Corinthians 7:1) This is the testimony of St. Paul and all those made holy by God's Holy Spirit. It has been expressed classically in the letter to the Ephesians.

We have been chosen in Christ "before the foundation of the world, that we should be holy and blameless before him." (Ephesians 1:4) In Christ "we have redemption through his blood, the forgiveness of our trespasses, according to the riches of his grace which he lavished upon us." (1:7-8)

For [God] has made known to us in all wisdom and insight the mystery of his will, according to his purpose which He set forth in Christ as a plan for the fulness of time, to unite all things in him, things in heaven and things on earth. [1:9-10]

We all "were dead through the trespasses" of sin following "the spirit that is now at work in the sons of disobediance. . . ; we all once lived in the passions of our flesh, following the desires of body and mind. . ." (2:2-3)

But God, who is rich in mercy, out of the great love with which he loved us, even when we were dead through our trespasses, made us alive together with Christ. . . . [2:4]

So, through Christ, we "have access in one Spirit to the Father." (2:18) We have "insight into the mystery of Christ. . . as it has now been revealed to his holy apostles and prophets by the Spirit." (3:4-5) We can "see what is the plan of the mystery hidden for ages in God who created all things." (3:9) We can be "strengthened with might through his Spirit in the inner man. . . that Christ may dwell in (our) hearts through faith; that. . . being rooted and grounded in love, (we) may have the power to comprehend with all the saints what is the breadth and length and height and depth, and to know the love of Christ which surpasses knowledge (and). . . be filled with all the fulness of God." (3:16-19) We can attain to "the knowledge of the Son of God, to mature manhood, to the measure of the stature of the fulness of Christ." (4:13) We can be liberated "so that we may no longer be children, tossed to and fro and carried about with every wind of doctrine, by the cunning of men, by their graftiness in deceitful wiles." (4:14) "Speaking the truth in love, we are to grow up in every way in him who is the head, into Christ." (4:15) We can "no longer live as the Gentiles do, in the futility of their minds,. . . .darkened in their understanding, alienated from the life of God because of the ignorance that is in them, due to their hardness of heart." (4:17) But, "as the truth is in Jesus," we can "put off our old nature which belongs to (our) former manner of life and is corrupt through deceitful lusts, and be renewed in the spirit of (our) minds, and put on the new nature, created after the likeness of God in true righteousness and holiness." (4:21-24) We can put away all falsehood, sinful anger, bitterness, clamor, wrath, immorality, impurity, covetousness, evil talk, darkness, disobedience, debauchery, foolishness "forgiving one another as God in Christ forgave" us. (4:32, cf. 5:3-6) We can "be imitators of God, as beloved children. And walk in love, as Christ has loved us and gave himself up for us." (5:1-2) We can, finally, "not grieve the Holy Spirit of God, in whom" we have been "sealed for the day of redemption." (4:30)

All of this is real. It is not exalted rhetoric, hyperbolic fantasy, exuberant nonsense. It is the immediate experience of the human person filled with the Spirit of God.

When we contemplate the indwelling of God's Spirit in man, its reality and its result, we are confronted with a question that has plagued all who have tried to analyze and explain it: What is the relationship between human nature and divine grace, between man's spirit and God's? The question is usually put this way: What comes first in the relationship between God and man—man's active openness to God's grace, or God's gracious action toward and in man? And, always the answer has been: God's gracious action is primary. But then, the reasoning has continued, must we not conclude logically that man's freedom in relation to God is for nothing? Must we not say that God chooses those whom he wills for salvation by pure predestination, and that everything in man's life depends exclusively upon the soverign election of God, without any participation or cooperation of man? Is not man a mere tool in God's hands, an impotent "mass of perdition" enslaved to the lusts of the flesh and the dust of the earth, whom God, if he so wills in his mercy, may save, but whom he may also as easily damn, and most properly so, through his just and righteous judgment? Do we not have to conclude that human nature and human freedom are without genuine significance in relation to God, because as God himself has said, "I will be gracious to whom I will be gracious, and will show mercy on whom I will show mercy." (Exodus 33:19, Romans 9:15-18)

The answer to these questions from the perspective of the spiritual tradition of the Eastern Orthodox Church is that they are wrongly placed, and there can be no right answer to a false question. How, for example, can one rightly answer the question whether the earth is flat or square, or whether the color of grass is purple or red? First, the question must be put in a way that renders it capable of proper response.

According to the spiritual tradition of the Eastern Church, any existential "opposition" between man's spirit and the Spirit of God is false. It supposes either that human nature can be free and active without the grace of God and that man, therefore, can somehow earn and merit salvation by his own energies and powers; or that human nature can in no way cooperate with divine grace, and that man's salvation and liberation is an act totally dependent on God's sovereign will without any effort or merit on man's part, making the human person a passive tool in God's hands.

This *either/or*, in the Eastern view, is a terrible mistake. Man's nature is never free and active in isolation; it is never "autonomous," having a "law" of its own. Man's nature by necessity, in its very being and reality, is either in union with the Spirit of God, and as such is free, authentic, with perfect self-determination; or else it is in union with evil and sin, and is unfree, inauthentic, captivated and enslaved by the dust and nothingness from which it is made. It is the grace of God, the indwelling of God's Spirit in man, which allows man to be man, to be free and active, to be involved authentically in his own salvation through genuine and free cooperation with God. This is the way that the well-known words of St. Paul in the letter to the Romans are normally interpreted in the Eastern perspective.

. . . I am carnal, sold under sin. I do not understand my own actions. For I do not do what I want, but I do the very thing I hate. Now if I do what I do not want. . . .it is no longer I that do it, but sin which dwells within me. . . .I can will what is right, but I cannot do it. For I do not do the good I want, but the evil I do not want is what I do. Now if I do what I do not want, it is no longer I that do it, but sin which dwells within me.

So I find it to be a law that when I want to do right, evil lies close at hand. For I delight in the law of God, in my inmost self, but I see in my members another law at war with the law of my mind and making me captive to the law of sin which dwells in my members. . . .[Romans 7:14-23]

. . . the law of the Spirit of life in Christ Jesus has set me free from the law of sin and death. . . . For those who live according to the flesh set their minds on the things of the flesh, but those who live according to the Spirit set their minds on the things of the Spirit. To set the mind on the flesh is death, but to set the mind on the Spirit is life and peace. For the mind that is set on the flesh is hostile to God. . . . and those who are in the flesh cannot please God.

But you are not in the flesh, if the Spirit of God really dwells in you. Any one who does not have the Spirit of Christ does not belong to him. But if Christ is in you, although your bodies are dead because of sin, your spirits are alive because of righteousness. . . .

. . . for if you live according to the flesh you will die, but if by the Spirit you put to death the deeds of the body you will live. For all who are led by the Spirit of God are sons of God. For you did not receive the spirit of slavery. . . but you have received the Spirit of sonship....it is the Spirit himself bearing witness with our spirit that we are children of God. . . . [Romans 8:2-16]

Thus, according to the apostolic teaching, human spirit is either captivated by the "law of sin and death," or liberated by the "law of the Spirit of life in Christ Jesus." It is never neutral. It is never "autonomous." But—and the *but* here is critical—the "law of the Spirit" does not destroy human nature and human freedom. On the contrary, it fills it and allows it to accomplish what it wills. It allows the person to set his or her mind on the things of the Spirit and to do them, to live according to the Spirit, which is life and peace.

This teaching of St. Paul is the New Covenant version of the fundamental choice offered to human beings by God, which was spoken of in the Law of the Old Covenant, the basic choice which has no third possibility:

. . . I have set before you this day life and good, death and evil. If you obey the commandments of the Lord your God which I command you this day, by loving the Lord your God, by walking in his ways, and by keeping his commandments and his statutes and his ordinances, then you shall live. . . .But if your heart turns away, and you will not hear, but are drawn away to worship other gods and serve them, I declare to you this day, that you shall perish. . . .I call heaven and earth to witness against you this day, that I have set before you life and death, blessing and curse; therefore choose life, that you and your descendants may live, loving the LORD your God, obeying his voice, and cleaving to him. . . . [Deuteronomy 30:15-20]

What is given here in the Law is the Old Covenant version of the fundamental law given to human persons in creation when "God created man in his own image," (Genesis 1:27) For human beings were made to commune with God and with all of creation, with every tree in the garden, with the tree of life. They were forbidden only to eat—or even to touch—the "tree of the knowledge of good and evil," which according to the fathers means to enter into experiential communion with evil, for if he does so, he surely "shall die." (Genesis 2:15 ff.) This means that evil itself destroys, wickedness corrupts, sin kills. For God did not say, "Eat of this tree and *I will kill you.*" He said, ". . .in the day that you eat of it *you shall die.*" The church tradition sees in this divinely inspired story the same truth the Law proclaims and the apostle defends; that sin is enslavement and death; a "dehumanization" and "brutalization" (the expressions of St. Athanasius); a rejection of man's true humanity; an abdication and rejection of man's kingship, dominion, and self-control; a destruction and annihilation of man's true human nature as made in the image of God himself in perfect sovereignty and freedom. This is the teaching of the fathers, the saints, and the liturgy of the Church.

When thou didst create man by taking dust from the earth, and didst honor him with Thine own image, O God, Thou didst set him in a paradise of delight, promising him eternal life and the enjoyment of everlasting blessings in the observance of Thy commandments.

But when man disobeyed Thee, the true God who had created him, and was deceived by the guile of the serpent, becoming subject to death by his own transgressions, Thou O God . . . .didst send him forth from paradise into this world, returning him to the earth from he was taken, yet providing for him the salvation of regeneration through Thy Christ Himself.

For Thou didst not turn Thyself away forever from Thy creature, whom Thou hadst made, O Good One, ...through the tender compassion of Thy mercy. Thou didst visit him in various ways: Thou didst send prophets, . . . Thou didst give the law. . . . Thou didst appoint angels. . .And when the fulness of time had come, Thou didst speak to us through Thy Son Himself. . . .

[The Son Who is]. . . The Living Word, The True God, The Eternal Wisdom, The Life, The Sanctification, The Power, The True Light, through Whom the Holy Spirit was revealed, Who is The Spirit of Truth, The Gift of divine Sonship, the pledge of future inheritance, the first-fruit of eternal blessings, the life-creating power, the fountain of sanctification, through Whom every creature of reason and understanding worship Thee and always sing to Thee a hymn of glory. . . .(Eucharistic Prayer, *Liturgy of St. Basil*)

It is the doctrine of the Scriptures and the saints that human nature, with its reason and understanding, is made for communion with God. If human beings lose communion with God, they become unreasonable and ignorant. They become irrational beasts, animals, if not demons. In order to be human, men and women must choose life and do good. They must not turn away from God, or be drawn away by the voice of the serpent. They must not taste or touch evil through direct communion with sin. They must set their minds not on the flesh, but on the Spirit of life, for to set the mind on the flesh is death, but to set the mind on the Spirit of God is life and peace.

The point here is clear: If men and women are free at all, if they are authentically human, it is only because of the Spirit of God in them. Without the Spirit, they cease to be human and are not free. This freedom of true and genuine humanity in communion with God is given to humanity in Christ and the Church. For as it is written:

". . . you will know the truth and the truth will make you free. . . ."
Truly, truly, I say to you, everyone who commits sin is a slave to sin.
The slave does not continue in the house forever; the Son continues
forever. So if the Son makes you free, you will be free indeed. [*John*
8:32, 34-36]

Now the Lord is the Spirit, and where the Spirit of the Lord is, there is
freedom. And we all with unveiled face, beholding the glory of the
Lord, are being changed. . .from one degree of glory to another; for
this comes from the Lord who is the Spirit. [*2 Corinthians 3:17-18*]

God has made human beings to be his children, not his slaves, puppets, or playthings. God's greatest gift to his children is freedom, the "glorious liberty of the children of God." (Romans 8:21) God's children live by the law of the Spirit which is the "law of liberty." (James 1:25, 2:12) They live in communion with God through Christ in the Spirit. Thus, it is tragically wrong to oppose human freedom to divine grace, simply because without God's grace there is no freedom for human beings. But when a person is full of grace, he is liberated indeed. His acts become his own authentic acts, in perfect self-determination, because of the grace of the Spirit of God. This is exactly what is meant when Christ says, "with God all things are possible." (Matthew 10:27) And "all things are possible to him who believes." (Matthew 9:23) And "without me you can do nothing." (John 15:5) And "with God all things are possible to you." (Matthew 17:20) This also is what is meant when the Apostle Paul says, "I can do all things in Him Who strengthens me." (Philippians 4:13) And in the same letter: "Therefore, my beloved. . .work out your own salvation with fear and trembling; for God is at work in you, both to will and to work for His good pleasure." (Philippians 2:12-13)

In every case, the "I" and the "you" are not suppressed or destroyed by the power of God. They are saved and preserved in their full integrity and freedom by God's presence. It is not as if God by his grace "takes over" in human beings, acting "from the outside," forcing himself on his creatures as a slavemaster controls his slaves, or as a machine operator operates his machines. It is not as if God captivates a man's being and life, destroying the freedom of human spirit and overpowering human nature by the power of his divinity. The opposite is true. When a man is not in union with God, he is enslaved and manipulated by the powers of evil and he loses his god-like dignity and freedom.

To put it another way, God's Spirit is not the removal of the human spirit. God's power is not the cessation of human power. God's activity is not the suppression of human activity. God's grace is not a divine "possession" or "captivity" of a man's being. Only evil can possess and captivate. God can only give freedom and liberate. To be "full of grace" is not to be "possessed" by God, blindly directed and passively moved by divine force. God's grace does not make a man do what he does not will to do. The evil spirits and the "elemental powers" of graceless existence do that. God's grace allows a man to be and do what he wants to be and do, in the full integrity of his own personal and spiritual being made in the image of God. God's Spirit gives a man "self-control." (Galatians 5:22, 2 Timothy 1:7) But self-control is possible only when one is obedient to God and lives in union with him in the Spirit. The only alternative to such a life is beastly and demonic existence—one cannot really call it "life"—through the loss of self-control in slavery to the fleshly passions and carnal lusts of a creation stripped of divine grace. On this point, the elder Silouan of Mt. Athos has written:

We all suffer here on earth and seek freedom, but few there are who know the meaning of freedom and where it is to be found.

I too want freedom, and seek it night and day. I learned that freedom is with God and is given of God to humble hearts who have repented and sacrificed their wills to Him.

The Lord does not desire the death of a sinner and on him who repents He bestows the grace of the Holy Spirit which gives peace to the soul and freedom for the mind and heart to dwell in God. When the Holy Spirit forgives our sins we receive freedom to pray to God with undistracted mind, and we can freely think on God and live serene and joyous in Him. And this is true freedom. But without God there can be no freedom, for the enemy [i.e. the devil] agitates the soul with evil thoughts.

O my brethren the world over, repent while there is time. God mercifully awaits our repentance. And all heaven and all the saints look for our repentance. And God is love, so the Holy Spirit in the saints is Love. Ask, and the Lord will forgive. And when you receive forgiveness of sins there will be joy and gladness in your souls, and the grace of God will enter in your souls, and you will cry: "This is true freedom. True freedom is in God and of God."

The grace of God does not take away freedom, but merely helps man to fulfill God's commandments. Adam knew grace, but he could still exercise his will. Thus too the angels abide in the Holy Spirit and yet are not deprived of free will.

This is true freedom—to be in God. I did not know this before. . . . The Lord wants us to love one another: in this—in love toward God and our fellow-man—lies freedom. In this lies both freedom and equality. . . . (Wisdom from Mt. Athos)

To the extent that a person knows the truth and does good in his life, he or she is free and is united with God in the Spirit. To the extent that a person is in darkness and does evil, his or her freedom is bound by sinful passions. A man may "choose evil," but when he does so, he surrenders his God-given freedom and makes himself a slave to the powers of evil. A man may be in slavery to sin because of his involvement in a sinful culture and society, the sins of others and the sins of the world. In this sense he is a victim who needs to be saved. But, once more, to the extent that a person is liberated from darkness and sin, he is saved by the grace of the Spirit of God.

In human salvation—which is liberation for life in the freedom, truth, and righteousness of God; a dynamic and ongoing condition of life—humanity is "saved" by God's Spirit allowing human spirit to be subject to a person's own self-determination in union with God. In the human condition of salvation, God's action is certainly "first," and the initiative is always his. God is the Creator, man is the creature. God is the Archetype, man is the image. God is the Savior, man is the saved. God is the Giver, man is the receiver.

But while the real distinction between God and humankind remains and will remain forever, with God having absolute priority, there can be no separation or division between what is of God and what is of humanity in the union. When the union between God and human beings is analyzed and explained, logically and ontologically, God is "first." But chronologically, it cannot be said who is "first." Temporal categories simply do not apply. God does not act first in a moment of time. Nor does man approach first by his own effort. The mystery of salvation and grace, of human spirit becoming "one spirit" with God's, does not allow for a temporal "first" and "second." Such an analysis is fallacious. For the act of communion between God and humankind is one a temporal act, as much humanity's as it is God's. But it is humanity's because it is God's through the gift of his Spirit. For, as Christ has said, "Without me, you can do nothing." (John 15:5) This is the mystery of grace, of communion between God and human beings. If this were not true, there would be no worth to human life, no value to human achievements, no meaning to human understanding and doing of the truth. There would be no sense to man's being made in the image and likeness of God, no sense to God's giving the Law, no sense to God's salvation in Christ and the Spirit. Indeed, there would be no sense to anything at all. Man would himself be god, fully capable of achieving divinity in and by himself, or by merely using God and his grace as a means and a tool, subject to the sovereign exercise of man's autonomous free will (an absurdity on the basis of the facts and an impiety on the basis of the faith). Or man would merely be God's plaything, with God choosing to save some people and to condemn others, according to his own autocratic decision. The explanation that all people deserve damnation, but that God in his mercy saves some, without or even against their will, is no explanation at all. It produces more problems than it solves, for it makes human existence a play written by God in which the actors are without personal integrity and freedom, and, therefore, without value and worth in their own right, indeed without any *life* in themselves in any real way. The only proper understanding of the matter, borne out by the way we really are and act, as well as how God has shown himself to be and to act, is that we are free, and that our salvation is the proper exercise of our created freedom through union with God, which "union" is radically dependent upon God in his action in us through his Word and Spirit.

It is worthwhile to consider more carefully the meaning of salvation in the traditional Christian view. Salvation basically means the power for human beings to know the truth, to do good with their lives, and to live forever in loving communion with God, their fellow creatures, and all creation. Humanity, to be saved (to live authentically), must therefore be free. Each person must be the personal living temple of God in the Spirit. But a person who is enslaved to the law of sin and death is not free and cannot bring about his freedom by his own power, for he has no such power. This is the human problem, its tragic condition: Humanity must be free, but human beings are not free and they cannot free themselves. This is why the eternal Logos and Son of God, one of the Holy Trinity, must be incarnate and become human for man's salvation and liberation. The Son of God—the express image of God the Father—must recapitulate in his own person every condition of humanity, to liberate it and to set it free from slavery to the law of sin and death. The incarnation of God in human flesh is essential for human salvation because it is human beings who must be saved. It is they who must turn to God and reflect the divine nature. It is they who must be "the dwelling place of God in the Spirit."

For this to happen, God cannot simple will it. He cannot, sit in his holy heaven and merely "pronounce" salvation from on high by divine fiat. For it is human beings in their sovereign freedom who must be saved; who must turn to God in the full integrity of his own human freedom, the freedom given to them by the Spirit of God dwelling within them. So God had to become man. The Word had to "become flesh". The Son of the Father had to become the son of Mary. He had to assume the fulness of human nature. He had to be found in human likeness in the form of a servant. He had to be the obedient one, anointed with the Spirit of God. He had to take on the sin of the world. He has to become a curse to destroy the curse. He had to become sin to restore righteousness. He had to become dead to make all things alive once more with God. He had to do this precisely to save, preserve, and empower human freedom—to restore human liberty from within, in spirit and in truth, by the unction of the Holy Spirit. He had to do it because this is what salvation is.

For this very reason, the fathers of the Church fought and died first of all for the true *divinity* of the Son of God. If Christ is not divine, humanity is not saved, for human nature is not restored in Christ and by Christ to full communion with God. Humanity is not liberated in him by becoming once more through him the image of God, the perfect reflection of the Father in the Spirit. Second, the fathers fought and died for the true *humanity* of Christ, for his true human soul and body, for his true and genuine human freedom and will, for if Christ is not "wholly man"—like us in every respect except sin (Cf. Hebrews 2)—we are not truly saved, for our human nature, with its rational soul and body, its mind and heart, its freedom and will, is not restored to full communion with God in its complete human integrity. It is still held captive to sin and death.

Only God can save. But it is human beings, in their freedom, who must be saved. So God becomes man so that in Christ, in the perfect freedom and integrity of his humanity, the divine and the human might be brought together once more in union, cooperation, and mutual participation in one "lived reality"—"without separation or division" (as the 4th Ecumenical Council in Chalcedon has said it), and also "without fusion or mixture" of what is of God and what is of man.

Taking this view of human salvation in Christ, we can see better how, by the grace of Christ, we are saved through communion with God in the Spirit. We are saved because our freedom is restored by the deified freedom of Christ's humanity, which becomes ours, once more by the Spirit of Christ. We are saved because in Christ we become the "dwelling place of God in the Spirit"—without separation or division, and without fusion or mingling, between what is of God and what is human. This is the mystery of salvation: God and humankind in perfect union, with the full integrity of Creator and creature, Archetype and image, Savior and saved, absolutely preserved. And yet, with the union so full and complete and perfect that in the "lived reality," God's action and human action are existentially one, and can in no way be divided.

His divine power has granted to us all things that pertain to life and godliness, through the knowledge of him who called us to his own glory and excellence, by which he has granted to us his precious and very great promises, that through these you may escape from the corruption that is in the world because of passion, and become partakers of the divine nature. For this very reason make every effort to supplement your faith with virture, and virtue with knowledge, and knowledge with self-control, and self-control with steadfastness, and steadfastness with godliness, and godliness with brotherly affection, and brotherly affection with love. For if these things are yours and abound, they keep you from being ineffective or unfruitful in the knowledge of our Lord Jesus Christ. [2 Peter 1:3-8]

These scriptural words are confirmed in many different ways in the writings of the saints. We can offer virtually limitless examples.

When He became incarnate and was made man He recapitulated in himself the long history of man, summing up and giving salvation in

*order that we might receive again in Christ Jesus what
we had lost in Adam, that is, the image and likeness of God.* [*St.
Irenaeus,* Against the Heresies)

*. . . The Word was made flesh in order to offer this body for all, and
that we partaking of His Spirit might be deified, a gift we could
otherwise not have gained than by His clothing Himself in our
created body, for hence we derive our name of "men of God" and
"men in Christ." But as we, by receiving the Spirit, do not lose our
proper human nature, so the Lord, when He was made man for
us. . .was no less God; for He was not lessened by the envelopement
of the body, but rather deified it and rendered it immortal.* [*St.
Athanasius,* Defense of the Nicene Definition)

*. . .He was transfused throughout our nature that our nature by this
transfusion of the Divine might become itself divine, rescued as it
was from death, and put beyond the reach of the caprice of the
antagonist* [*i.e. the devil*]. *For His return from death becomes to our
mortal race the commencement of our return to the immortal life.*
[*St. Gregory of Nyssa,*   The Great Catechism)

*He who gives riches becomes poor, for He assumes the poverty of
my flesh that I might assume the riches of His Divinity. He that is full
empties Himself. . . .that I may share in His fulness. What is the
riches of His goodness? What is this mystery around me? I had a
share in the Image, but I did not keep it. He partakes of my flesh that
He might both save the image and make my flesh immortal. . . .*

*Such is the paschal msytery; such are the mysteries foreshadowed in
the Law and fulfilled by Christ. . .the Perfecter of the Holy Spirit
who by His passion taught us how to suffer, and by His glorification
grants us to be glorified with Him.* [*St. Gregory the Theologian,* The
Second Easter Oration)

The fact that it is impossible to introduce any sort of temporal
primacy into the gracious union between God and humankind is
seen very clearly in a human person's act of prayer. A person prays

because he or she is inspired by God's Spirit to do so. No one can call Jesus "Lord" except by the Holy Spirit. (Cf. 1 Corinthians 12:3) And no one can call God "Father" unless the Spirit of God inspires him.

So with us; when we were children, we were slaves to the elemental spirits of the universe. But when the time had fully come, God sent forth his Son, born of woman, born under the law, to redeem those who were under the law, so that we might be made sons. And because you are sons, God has sent the Spirit of his Son into our hearts, crying, "Abba! Father!" So through God you are no longer a slave, but a son. . . . [Galatians 4:3-7]

When we cry "Abba! Father!" it is the Spirit himself bearing witness with our spirit that we are children of God. . . .

Likewise the Spirit helps us in our weakness; for we do not know how to pray as we ought, but the Spirit himself intercedes for us with sighs too deep for words. And he who searches the heart of men knows what is the mind of the Spirit, because the Spirit intercedes for the saints according to the will of God. [Romans 8:15-16, 26-27]

Thus, in the act of prayer, the human spirit and God's Spirit become "one spirit" as a man or woman is enabled to confess Jesus as Lord, and through him to address the heavenly and almighty God with the name of "Father." How does one understand and explain the action? Must we pray in order to have the Spirit? Or must we have the Spirit in order to pray? Or is it not true that we pray to have the Spirit, and that our very act of prayer is proof that the Spirit of God is already in us enabling us to call upon God—even to send us his Spirit—through the Spirit that is already in us. Is this not the paradoxical answer which the mysterious intercommunion in grace between God and humankind, and humankind and God, requires?

Let us see how the saints speak on this point, for their language is paradoxical indeed. They claim, for example, that one must make great effort in prayer so that the grace of God and the indwelling of the Holy Spirit can be "acquired" and "achieved." But then they go on to say that this very effort is possible only by the grace of God's indwelling Spirit. They teach also that one must have faith, love, grace, and virtue in order to be successful in prayer, and that prayer without these spiritual possessions is impossible and without effect. But they go on to say that faith and love, grace, and virtue are the merciful gifts of God, which human beings cannot merit or deserve by any kind of spiritual works, not even prayer; while still claiming that a person receives these divine gifts primarily by—and not without—praying! Thus, the saints seem to say that one must have faith in order to receive faith, good works in order to do good works, virtue in order to be virtuous, grace in order to receive grace, and the gift of prayer in order to pray, which gift itself is received primarily through praying! Then the fathers say that while we pray to receive God's Spirit, but can only pray if the Spirit is already in us, that we also need not pray any longer when the Spirit is in us because this itself is the purpose and goal of prayer and when this occurs, all prayer is accomplished!

If the spiritual life of man's gracious communion with God in Christ and the Spirit did not have a "logics" of its own, fully adequate to the mystical reality of man's spirit becoming "one spirit" with God, all of this would be utterly illogical and absurd—as indeed it is to those who have not the "mind of the Spirit," which comes through the existential experience of communion with God. For as St. Paul has said, "The unspiritual man does not receive the gifts of the Spirit of God, for they are folly to him, and he is not able to comprehend them because they are spiritually discerned," while the spiritual human being, the saint, has received the "Spirit which is from God" and so can "understand the gifts bestowed on us by God" and can grasp and appreciate as well the manner of their bestowal. (Cf. 1 Corinthians 2:10-16) Thus, we have as a classical example of such a paradoxical teaching on prayer, the following words of Saint Seraphim of Sarov (d. 1833):

. . .*every virtuous act done for Christ's sake gives us the grace of the Holy Spirit, but most of all is this given through prayer; for prayer is always in our hands as an instrument for acquiring the grace of the Spirit.*

. . . .prayer is always possible for everyone, rich and poor, noble and simple, strong and weak, healthy and suffering, righteous and sinful. Great is the power of prayer; most of all does it bring the Spirit of God and easiest of all is it to exercise. Truly, in prayer it is granted to us to converse with our God and Life-creating God and Saviour, but even here we must pray only until God the Holy Spirit descends on us in measures of His heavenly grace known to Him. When He comes to visit us, we must cease to pray. How can we pray "cleanse us from all impurity and save our souls O Good One," when He has already come to us to save us who trust in Him and call on His holy name in truth, that humbly and with love we may receive Him, the Comforter, in the chamber of our souls, hungering and thirsting for His coming? (Conversation with Motovilov)

How are we to understand these bold words? Does that holy man really say that we are to pray for the Spirit, on our own, and then when the Spirit comes we are to stop praying? I think, considering the whole of Saint Seraphims's life and teaching, as well as that of the many other masters of prayer, that this is not what the holy father is trying to say. Rather, the invocation of the Holy Spirit is basic to our prayer. We always begin with the prayer to the Holy Spirit, which is made by the grace of the Spirit already in us—as St. Augustine put it when he said that the seeking of God is the sign that the seeker has already been found by him. But—and this is clear in the Eastern tradition, both in personal and liturgical prayer—once the Holy Spirit has been invoked to "come and abide in us," one truly ceases to pray *to* the Holy Spirit, but prays *in* the Holy Spirit to God the Father through his Son Jesus Christ as the continual and abiding condition of his entire being and life. For Saint Seraphim himself was "aglow with the Spirit" because he was truly "constant in prayer" (Romans 12:11-12), following the apostolic command to "pray without ceasing." (1 Thessalonians 5:17) What "ceases" with the indwelling of the Holy Spirit is not prayer as such, but prayer *to* the Spirit. For when man's spirit is "one spirit" with the Spirit of God, then man's whole life becomes perpetual and ceaseless prayer to God the Father, through Christ the Son, in the Holy Spirit. We see this not only in Saint Seraphim's life, but in the lives and teachings of all of

God's saints, not *virtually* all, or *almost* all, but *literally* all without exception.

Prayer is spiritual breathing. In praying we breathe by the Holy Spirit: "pray in the Holy Spirit." [Jude 20] And so all churchly prayers are the breath of the Holy Spirit. . . .

In churchly prayers and hymns. . .there moves the Spirit of Truth. Everything contradictory and blasphemous which comes into our heads from the outside is from the devil, the slanderer, the father of lies. Prayers and hymns are the breath of the Holy Spirit.

Do you not know that during prayer the Father, the Son, and the Holy Spirit are in you and you in them?

Prayer is the breath of the soul as air is the natural breath of the body. We breathe spiritually by the Holy Spirit. You cannot say a single word of prayer from your whole heart [even of invocation of the Spirit Himself] without the Holy Spirit. In praying. . .you converse with the Lord and if your spiritual lips are opened by faith and love, you, as it were, breathe in from the Spirit at that very moment the spiritual blessings are requested through the Holy Spirit.

When you stand up to pray, burdened by many sins and filled with despair, begin to pray with hope with a burning spirit, remembering that the Spirit Himself helps us in our weaknesses, "making intercessions for us with groanings too deep for words." When you will have remembered with faith this action of within us of God's Spirit. . .you will have peace in your heart, a sweetness, a justification, a joy in the Holy Spirit [and] you will cry out with words in the heart: "Abba! Father!" [Father John of Cronstadt, d. 1908, My Life in Christ)

This is also the teaching of the great nineteenth century Russian master of prayer, Bishop Theophan the Recluse. It is impossible to grasp mentally, with Aristotelian logic; but the witness itself is bold and clear, for as Theophan has said, "Theorists are greatly occupied by the question of the relationship between grace and free will. For anyone who has grace within him, this question is resolved by practical experience. . . For him, this Truth is more evident. . . than any experience of his external life. . . ."[1]

Prayer is the test of everything; prayer also is the source of everything; prayer is the driving force of everything; prayer is also the director of everything. If prayer is right, everything is right. For prayer will not allow anything to go wrong.

If you are not successful in your prayer, do not expect success in anything. Prayer is the root of all.

"Prayer without ceasing," St. Paul writes. . .[Thessalonians 5:7]. And in other epistles, he commands: "Praying with all supplications in the Spirit." [Ephesians 6:18] "Continue in prayer. . ." [Colossians 4:2] "Continuing constant in prayer." [Romans 12:12] Also the Saviour teaches us the need for constancy and persistency in prayer. . . .

It is clear from this that unceasing prayer is not an accidental prescription, but the essential characteristic of the Christian spirit.

We are also taught that every Christian is the "temple of God" in which "dwelleth the Spirit of God." [1 Corinthians 3:16, 6:19; Romans 8:9]

It is the Spirit always present and pleading in him that prays within him "with groanings that cannot be uttered" [Romans 8:26], and so teaches him how to pray without ceasing.

The very first action of God's grace in the turning of the sinner to God manifests itself by the bending of the mind and heart toward God.

1. *The Art of Prayer*, Igumen Chariton, ed.

When later, by repentance and dedication of his life to God, the grace of God which acted from without descends on him and remains within him through the sacraments, then the turning of the mind and heart to God, which is the essence of prayer, will also become unchangeable and permanent in him.

The turning is made evident in different degrees, and, like any other gift, must be renewed. It is refreshed according to its kind: by the effort of prayer and especially by patient and attentive practice of churchly prayers.

Pray without ceasing, exert yourself in prayer, and you will achieve incessant prayer, which will act of itself in the heart without special effort.

The whole of life, in all its manifestations must be permeated by prayer. And its secret is love for the Lord. As a bride, loving the bridegroom, is not separated from him in remembrance and feeling, so the soul, united with God in love, remains in constancy with Him, directing fervent appeals to Him from the heart. "He that is joined unto the Lord is one spirit with Him." [Theophan the Recluse][1]

In the spiritual tradition of the Church, the perfection of human persons as the "temples of the Holy Spirit" (1 Corinthians 6:9), rooted and grounded in prayer, consists in being in the continual movement of growth in communion with God. The content of this dynamic union with God in the Spirit is existentially expressed in personal growth in the grace and holiness of God. It may as well be defined negatively as simple "not sinning." To the extent that one is in communion with God through Christ by the Holy Spirit, one literally cannot sin. The purpose of prayer is to insure that the person will remain in such a spiritual condition, and so will be invulnerable to the temptations of the devil. This is the teaching of Saint John:

No one who abides in him sins; no one who sins has either seen him

1. *The Act of Prayer*, Igumen Chariton, ed.

or known him. . . .No one born of God commits sin; for God's
nature abides in him and he cannot sin because he is born of
God. . . .And by this we know that he abides in us, by the Holy
Spirit which he has given us. [*I; John 3:6, 9, 24*]

Prayer is the continual state of being "born of God," in the Spirit,
the condition of life in which sin becomes impossible for the human
person. If we had to describe how this happens, according to the
testimony of the saints, we would do so in the following way. The
temptation to evil enters everyone's life. Being tempted should not
be confused or equated with sinning, for even Christ was tempted:
"For because he himself has suffered and been tempted, he is able to
help those who are tempted." (Hebrews 2:18) When the inevitable
temptation comes, it enters the person's mind, heart, and body. If it
is allowed to work in a person's members, it will certainly produce its
evil fruit in that person's life. The temptation must be overcome, and
it must be rejected and conquered immediately, at its first entrance.
(This is how the fathers, Nilus of Sinai, for example, interpret such
lines in the Psalter as the following, which shock and embarrass
many Christians: "Blessed is he who takes your little ones and dash-
es them against the rocks!" Psalm 137:9). If the temptation to evil is
not overcome immediately, if it is "taken in" and "played with"—if
not actually accepted and cultivated—it will certainly lead to sin.
The temptation, however, can only be overcome by grace, by the
power of God, of Christ and the Spirit. Temptation cannot possibly
be overcome by "will power." A person who tries to overcome
temptation by will power always fails ultimately, and not seldom
after great mental, spiritual, and bodily anguish. Evil must be
conquered by the grace of God, by the power of God's Spirit
working in the person. Prayer guarantees this presence of the Spirit's
grace and power in a person's mind, heart, and body.

But how does this grace work in overcoming temptation? It is
important to understand it, because not a few people think that
divine grace acts like magic, and they expect it to do so when they are
tempted. They expect to pray, "God help me!" and have the Holy
Spirit appear and snatch them from the clutches of evil like the hero
in a melodrama. They expect God to act as a *deus ex machina*,

sending his powerful Spirit to crush man's evil foes. But the saints witness that it does not happen this way, and the ill-informed expectation of some people that it should happen this way is the cause of no little anguish and frustration in their lives.

How then, does prayerful deliverance from temptation work? The saints show that it is something like this: The temptation comes. Its coming signals and activates a person's mind, heart, and body to pray to God. Through prayer, the Spirit is present, unifying that person's powers and uniting him or her wholly in God through Christ. (I believe that this happens, when prayer is genuine and true, even when it is not Christians who are praying.) Being thus in union with God, the person literally cannot sin, not because God snatches him or her away from evil, or crushes evil for him or her through some sort of brute divine force, but because the person, inspired and enlightened by prayer, sees the evil for what it is in the light of divine wisdom. The person sees the evil as powerless and foolish, the object of sadness and mourning. The person sees, as well, the fundamental and God-given beauty and goodness of the one through whom the temptation to evil comes—for no evil is presented to human beings except through that which is fundamentally good. This does not mean, as some teach, that evil always appears *sub specie boni*, that is, under the aspect and appearance of being something good. It means rather that evil is always and of necessity a perversion, corruption, and aberration of something good. Thus, the temptation to sin, rather than being externally expelled, rejected, or crushed, becomes itself the cause and "stimulus" of the person's goodness and virtue. The person is tempted. He or she prays in the Spirit; and is in union with God filled with wisdom and truth, with light and love. In such a condition, the person "disarms" and "defuses" the temptation to evil by actually "transforming" it into the cause of deeper and greater wisdom and virtue, more compassionate mercy, greater self-emptying love.

Thus, for example, a person is tempted to anger or lust, to slander or gossip, to cruelty or contempt. The temptation comes always in someone or something. The temptation is always to return evil for evil or to destroy something good. But a person filled with the Spirit will be immune to such action. The good object presented for evil use will be seen as good, beautiful, from God, to be loved, cared for, received with thanksgiving. And the evil object, presented as that to be treated with evil in return, will be seen as a "good thing" spoiled and harmed, and therefore not to be spoiled and harmed further by the return of evil, but rather to be treated with mercy and compassion, to be mourned and lamented, to be forgiven, to be helped, to be cared for, to be served in self-sacrificing love if only it could be purified, healed, and saved for life with God. This, I think, is how prayer in the Spirit delivers a person from evil. It makes the person "divine by grace" and enables that person to have a "divine reaction" to things, both good and evil, and to treat them in a way that will be for their own good, just as God does. A person in such a condition will not, and cannot, sin.

It is the human vocation to grow in the perfection of God forever. The perfection of God is absolute; superessential, superabundant, infinite, and inexhaustible. Human perfection is to grow in God's perfection, "to mature manhood, to the measure of the stature of the fulness of Christ." (Ephesians 4 : 13) It is to be in the dynamic process of "being changed in His likeness from one degree of glory to another" and "this comes from the Lord who is the Spirit." (2 Corinthians 3 : 18) This understanding of human life has been very clearly expressed by Saint Gregory of Nyssa in his mystical writings about a human being's communion with God within the life of the Christian Church. The following selection of texts from St. Gregory reveals how this process develops in man's spiritual experience of God in the Spirit.

The blessed and eternal being of God that surpasses all understanding contains all perfection within itself and cannot be limited. . . . When therefore it draws human nature to participate in its perfection, because of the divine transcendence it is always superior to our nature in the same degree. The soul grows by participation in that which transcends it ; and yet the perfection in which the soul participates remains ever the same. . . .

We see then [Christ] the Word, leading His bride up a rising staircase, as it were up to the heights of perfection. The Word sends first a ray of light through the windows of the Prophets and through the grill-work of the Law and the commandments.

Then He bids His bride to draw near to the Light and then to become beautiful by being transformed in the Light, into the form of the Dove [which is the Spirit of God.]

He. . .continues to draw her on to participate in transcendent Beauty as though she had never tasted of it. In this way her desire grows as she goes on. . .she always seems to be beginning anew.

Thus in a certain sense [human nature] is constantly being created, ever changing for the better in its growth in perfection. . .nor can its progressive growth in perfection be limited by any term.

Through all of this the bride emerges ever more perfect. . . .God comes to the soul, and the soul in turn is united with God. . .to Him who has transformed our human nature from the realm of shadowy appearances to that of ultimate truth. . . .

For surely nothing can surpass the joy of being within the Beloved when the Beloved is also within us.

He says: . . . . You were buried with me in baptism unto death, but you rose again and ascended into communion with my divinity. . .So rise up now. . .and go on. . .advancing and ever rising by active knowledge. . . .

So too, now, when the Word calls a soul that has advanced to come to Him, it is immediately empowered at His command and becomes what the Bridegroom wishes. It is transformed into something divine, and it is transformed from the glory in which it exists to a higher glory by a perfect kind of transformation. . . .

It is indeed through the Church that the manifold wisdom of God is made known. . . .how the Word becomes flesh, life is mingled with death, in his bruises our wound is healed, the infirmity of the cross destroys the power of the adversary [i.e. the devil], He Himself is both the purchaser and the price. . .He is in the throes of death and does not depart from life, He is sent into slavery, and remains the King.

And He made the church His body, and He builds it with love. . .until we all shall be united in one perfect man," unto the measure of the stature of the fulness of Christ." [Ephesians 4:13]

And so he who sees the Church looks directly at Christ—Christ building and increasing by addition of the chosen. . . .

The establishment of the Church is the re-creation of the world. In the Church there is a new heaven. . .a new firmament. . .a new earth. . . .Man is created once again, for by his rebirth from high he is renewed according to the image of his Creator. There is also a new light. . .there are many stars. . .called by name, for their names. . .have been written in heaven. . . .

So too, anyone who looks upon the universe of this new creation reflected in the Church, can see in it Him who is all in all. . .Him [who]gave His disciples divine glory when He said to them: "Receive ye the Holy Spirit." [John 20:22]

And now that His human nature has been glorified by the Spirit, this participation in the glory of the Spirit is communicated to all who are united with Him. . . . [On the Canticle of Canticles)

When God acts to bring human persons into ever-more-perfect union with himself through his Word and the Holy Spirit, he comes first with his gracious gifts to creation. The first gift of God is creation itself, God's gift of sharing his divine being and life. The manifold gifts of God's Spirit in creation are crowned with the making of human beings in God's own image and likeness, with each person being absolutely unique, with his or her own proper talents and gifts. The personal gifts of God to his individual creatures include all the faculties of body and soul, as well as the particular conditions of life best suited to the individual's needs and requirements for salvation as provided by God according to the inscrutable wisdom of his gracious and merciful providence. God knows what is best for each person and does what is best, given the facts of evil and sin, which are not of his making.

And remember Thyself O Lord, all those whom we have not remembered. . . .since Thou knowest the name and age of each, even from his mother's womb. . . .

Be all things to all men, O Thou who knowest each man and his request, his home and his need. . . .

Receive us all into Thy kingdom, showing us to be sons of the light and sons of the day. Grant us Thy peace and Thy love, O Lord our God, for Thou hast given all things unto us. [*Divine Liturgy of St. Basil*]

God has given all things to his creatures, not merely "in general," but specifically, to each one individually, as the best possible gifts and conditions for life and salvation. Everything a person has—his or her unique being and life, his or her unique personal characteristics, his or her unique place and position, his or her unique talents, and gifts and possessions—are all provided by God. They are the gifts of God's Spirit to be received and used as the means for perfection and life in union with God, according to the ways Gods has provided.

Within the life of the Church, for those who have been given the possibility to live this life on earth by the will and mercy of God, there are particular gifts and powers given by God's Spirit for the use of human beings in building up the Body of Christ, for witnessing to the truth and love of God's Kingdom, and for growing in perfection to mature personhood in Christ. These are the specific gifts of God's Spirit enumerated in the apostolic Scriptures:

Now there are varieties of gifts, but the same Spirit; and there are

varieties of service, but the same Lord; and there are varieties of
working, but it is the same God who inspires them all in every one.
To each is given the manifestation of the Spirit for the common
good. To one is given through the Spirit the utterance of wisdom,
and to another the utterance of knowledge according to the same
Spirit, to another faith by the same Spirit, to another gifts of healing
by the one Spirit, to another the working of miracles, to another
prophecy, to another the ability to distinguish between spirits, to
another various kinds of tongues, to another the interpretation of
tongues. All these are inspired by one and the same Spirit, who
apportions to each one individually as he wills. [1 Corinthians
12:4-11]

The same teaching has been given by the Staretz Silouan in our
own time:

The Holy Spirit sets us all on different paths: one person lives a life
of silent solitude in the desert; another prays for mankind; still
another is called to minister to Christ's flock; to a fourth it is given to
comfort or preach to the suffering; while yet another serves his
neighbor by his goods or by the fruits of his labors—and all these are
gifts of the Holy Spirit given in various degrees. . . .

With society graduated on this earth there can be no equality; but
that is of no importance to the soul. Not everyone can be an emperor
or a prince; not everyone can be a patriarch or an abbot, or a leader;
but in every walk of life we can love God and be pleasing to Him, and
only this is important. And the man who loves God most in this
world will have the most glory in the Kingdom. He who loves most
will the most strongly yearn and reach for God, and be closest to
Him. Each will be glorified according to the measure of his love. And
I have discovered that love varies in strength. [Wisdom From Mount
Athos)

Not every member of the Church has all the gifts of the Spirit, for
they are given to individuals as God wills, according to their ability
and need to receive them for their own life and salvation, as well as

that of others around them. They are given that the Church may function properly and harmoniously for the common good of all, and that the "fruit of the Spirit" may be cultivated and produced in the life of God's people. (Cf. 1 Corinthians 12-14)

But I say, walk by the Spirit, and do not gratify the desires of the flesh. For the desires of the flesh are against the Spirit, and the desires of the Spirit are against the flesh; for these are opposed to each other, to prevent you from doing what you would. But if you are led by the Spirit you are not under the law. Now the works of the flesh are plain: immorality, impurity, licentiousness, idolatry, sorcery, enmity, strife, jealousy, anger, selfishness, dissension, party spirit, envy, drunkeness, carousing, and the like. I warn you, as I warned you before, that those who do such things shall not inherit the kingdom of God. But the fruit of the Spirit is love, joy, peace, patience, kindness, goodness, faithfulness, gentleness, self-control; against such there is no law. And those who belong to Christ Jesus have crucified the flesh with its passions and desires.
[*Galatians 5:16-24*]

Thus, the gifts of the Spirit of God are given that with them, the fruit of the Spirit can grow in human life. The Spirit's gifts are not ends in themselves, and by themselves they prove nothing about the holiness and virtue of those who possess them. Many of the saints were abundantly blessed with the gifts of God's Spirit, but the saints are saints not because of these gifts, but because of the fruit of the Holy Spirit manifested in their lives through the proper use of God's gifts. Many persons have received God's gifts and misused and abused them, even the special gifts of divine favor and power. As a witness to this we have the many parables of Christ about those who have been blessed by God, but have proved unworthy. And we have as well his words in the Sermon on the Mount where he says, not by their gifts, but "by their fruits you will know them." (Cf. Matthew 7: 16-20)

"Not every one who says to me, 'Lord, Lord,' shall enter the kingdom of heaven, but he who does the will of my Father who is in

heaven. On that day many will say to me, 'Lord, Lord, did we not prophesy in your name, and cast out demons in your name, and do many mighty works in your name?' And then will I declare to them, 'I never knew you; depart from me, you evildoers.' " [Matthew 7:21-23]

According to Christ's own teaching, therefore, there will be those who will have the gifts of the Holy Spirit, who will prophesy in God's name, who will cast out demons and do mighty works, but who themselves will be condemned by the Lord. How can we understand this? Why should God give his gifts to those who will not use them rightly for their own salvation? Whether or not we can understand, the fact remains that the Lord says that it is so, as does the apostle Paul. In the famous thirteenth chapter of his first letter to the Corinthians, Paul claims that people can have the gifts of tongues and prophecy, knowledge, faith and even generosity—and still be "nothing" and "profit nothing."

If I speak in the tongues of men and of angels, but have not love, I am a noisy gong or a clanging cymbal. And if I have prophetic powers, and understand all mysteries and all knowledge, and if I have all faith, so as to remove mountains, but have not love, I am nothing. If give away all I have, and if I deliver my body to be burned, but have not love, I gain nothing.

Love is patient and kind; love is not jealous or boastful; it is not arrogant or rude. Love does not insist on its own way; it is not irritable or resentful; it does not rejoice at wrong, but rejoices in the right. Love bears all things, believes all things, hopes all things, endures all things. [1 Corinthians 13:1-7]

In acknowledging the spiritual reality witnessed to in the Scriptures, we can go on to speculate how God's gifts can be misused without love. In the first place, God is not one to give gifts only if he is certain that his creatures will use them well. God does not give his gifts "on condition." He does not say, "I will give to you if you honor my gifts and use them in love for good." God just gives. That is his nature. He gives "asking nothing in return," just as he loves and does good and is merciful and kind even "to the ungrateful and the selfish," to those who do not love or do not do good as he has commanded. (Cf. Luke 6: 27-36)

If God would give only on condition of the good results of his giving, it is questionable whether he would have, or even could have, created the world at all. For indeed, who among men has responded—or can respond—fully and adequately to God's generosity, goodness, and love? Who can claim perfect productivity or fruit on a level equal to the gracious gifts of God's Spirit in creation and salvation through Christ? Only the saints could even begin to make such a claim, and they would be the last to do so. Witness the many testimonies of Saint Paul on this point. (For example, 1 Corinthians 15: 8-11; Ephesians 2:8, 1 Timothy 1: 12-16) Therefore, in the first place, we may say that God's generosity with the gifts of his Spirit in no way demonstrates that he gives them on condition of their good and proper use by human beings.

Second, some may beg God for his gifts, even the gifts of his Spirit, for their own vainglory, pride, and personal profit and prestige. Just as people may fast and pray and give alms only in order to be seen and so to be praised (Cf. Matthew 6:1-18), so some may preach the gospel "from envy and rivalry. . . out of partisanship . . . not sincerely. . . but in pretense" to bring praise to themselves or to make troubles for others, "like, so many, peddlars of God's word" and not for the glory of God and the good of his people. (Cf. Philippians 1:17-18; 2 Corinthians 2:17) And others also may simply preach for "shameful gain" or to be "domineering" and exercise authority over others. (Cf. 1 Peter 5: 1-3) This does not mean, necessarily, that those who act this way are devoid of the gifts of God's Spirit. On the contrary, they may be greatly talented and abundantly endowed with blessings. God may even be using them for his own glory and the salvation of others, who through them will really be instructed in God's word, healed by God's Spirit, and saved by God's gracious mercy and might. For Christ has said about the teachers whom he condemned: "Practice and observe whatever they tell you, but do not do what they do, for they preach and do not practice." (Matthew 23:3) Thus the teaching and the prophecy of certain men may truly be of the Spirit of God, while the teachers and prophesiers themselves may be lost. Even St. Paul was aware that this could happen, as he himself has said, "I pommel my own body and subdue it, lest after preaching to others, I (who have received many gifts of the Spirit through the revelation of Christ himself) may myself be disqualified." (1 Corinthians 9:27) And certainly it was also by God's Spirit that the people were instructed and cleansed by those who, according to the Lord, are to be condemned on the day of judgment. (Cf. Matthew 7:22-23)

In the view of the Scriptures and the saints, therefore, God can and does give his gifts to human beings, for their salvation and the salvation of others. But these spiritual gifts, like God's material gifts, can be received—like Christ himself in the eucharist—not "unto the forgiveness of sins, the healing of soul and body, and life everlasting," but rather "unto condemnation and judgment" to those who have received them in an unworthy manner. (Cf. Prayers before Holy Communion, Orthodox Divine Liturgy. Also 1 Corinthians 11:27-32, 13-14, passim.) The great fourteenth century Byzantine theologian, Nicholas Cabasilas, has written very clearly on this point:

It happened to some of the Corinthians while the apostles were still living. They were filled with the Spirit, they prophesied, spoke with tongues, and displayed other gifts; yet so far were they from being in a divine and spiritual state that they were beset with envy and untimely ambition, with strife and such like evils. For these things Paul blames them when he says, "you are of the flesh and are behaving like ordinary men." [1 Corinthians 3:3] *Even though they were spiritual in terms of participating in divine graces, yet it did not suffice them for casting out all evils from the soul.* [The Life in Christ, *Book IV*]

The saints also bear witness that some people can lust after the gifts, powers, and consolations of the Spirit in the same way that others lust after the gifts, powers, and consolations of the flesh. They do so for their own spiritual pleasure and satisfaction, and not for the production of virtue for God's sake and the sake of their fellowmen. These are they whom the spiritual masters accuse of "spiritual avarice," "spiritual luxury", "spiritual gluttony" (John of the Cross), and "spiritual hedonism." (Theophan the Recluse) Such people want to be holy so that *they* can be holy. They want to prophesy and do wonders so that *they* can do it. They want to be "spiritual" and "perfect" for their own egocentric benefit and pride. When they do wrong or are weak, they are sorrowful, not because of their sin, not because of the harm they do to others or the offense they have caused God and his creatures, but because *they* have fallen short and are not yet as holy as they desire to be! Such people are the sorriest of all God's creatures. For although they covet the gifts of God's Spirit, and may even receive many spiritual gifts—because of their public display of faith in Christ, so that God might uphold his honor and truth, and might, through them, lead others to himself—they themselves are still destined to hear the Lord's words on the dread day of judgment: "I never knew you; depart from me, you evildoers!" (Matthew 7:23)

The great spiritual master, John of the Cross, has described such people with startling clarity and power. He speaks, for example, of those who are childish and immature in their zeal for the things of the Spirit.

As these. . .feel themselves to be very fervent and diligent in spiritual things. . .there often comes to them. . .a certain kind of secret pride, whence they come to have some degree of satisfaction with their works and with themselves. And hence there comes to them likewise a certain desire, which is somewhat vain, and at times very vain, to speak of spiritual things in the presence of others. . . . In these persons the devil often increases the fervor that they have and the desire to perform these and other works more frequently, so that their pride and presumption may grow greater. For the devil knows quite well that these works and virtues which they perform are not only valueless to them, but even become vices in them. And such a degree of evil are some of these persons accustomed to reach that they would have none appear good except themselves; and thus, in deed and word, whenever the opportunity occurs, they condemn and slander them. . . .

Sometimes they are anxious that others shall realize how spiritual they are, to which end they occasionally give outward evidence thereof. . .in public rather than in secret. . .and are pleased that this should be noticed, and are often eager that it should be noticed more.

Many. . .have also at times great spiritual avarice. . . .They are disconsolate and querulous because they do not find in spiritual things the consolation that they would desire. Many can never have enough of listening to advice and spiritual precepts, and of possessing and reading many books. . .and they spend time on all these things rather than on works of mortification and the perfecting of the poverty of spirit which should be theirs.

For many of these lured by the sweetness and pleasure which they find in such [spiritual] exercises, strive more after spiritual sweetness then after spiritual purity and discretion, which is that which God regards and accepts. . . .

. . .attracted, exactly like beasts, by the desire and pleasure they find. . .they grow in vice rather than virtue, for to say the least, they are acquiring spiritual gluttony and pride. . . .

Through these efforts they lose true devotion and spirituality, which consists in perseverance, through patience and humility and mistrust of themselves, that they may please God alone. [Dark Night of the Soul, Bk. I]

John of the Cross also speaks specifically about what we would today call the "charismatic gifts" of the Spirit.

It is necessary also for us to treat of the. . .good things wherein the soul may rejoice. . .By this. . .we understand all the gifts and graces given by God which. . .are called gratis datae [gifts of grace]. Such as these are the gifts of wisdom and knowledge. . .and the graces whereof St. Paul speaks—namely faith, gifts of healing, the working

of miracles, prophecy, knowledge and discernment of spirits, inter-
pretation of works and likewise the gift of tongues.

Speaking now of these. . .gifts. . .I say that, in order to purge
ourselves of the vain joy in them, it is well to notice [their] two
benefits. . . .The temporal benefits are the healing. . . , the
receiving of sight. . . , the raising of the dead, the casting out devils,
prophesying. . . .The spiritual and eternal benefit is that God is
known and served through these good works by him that performs
them, or by those in whom, or in whose presence, they are
performed.

. . .without the second kind of benefit, they are of little or no
importance to man, since they are not in themselves a means of
uniting the soul with God, as love is. And these. . .works and graces
may be performed by those who are not in a state of grace or love,
even if they truly give thanks and attribute their gifts to God. . .or
whether they perform them falsely, through the agency of the
devil. . .or by means of other secrets of nature.

A person, then, should rejoice, not when he has such graces and
makes use of them, but when he reaps from them the second spiritual
fruit, namely that of serving God in them with true love, for herein is
the fruit of eternal life.

For these reasons our Savior reproved the disciples who were
rejoicing because they cast out devils. . .[cf, Luke 10 : 20] By this it is
understood that a man should not rejoice except when he is walking
in the way of life, which he may do by performing good works in
love. . .in this manner the will is united with God. . . .

. . .it is to be understood that the evil of this rejoicing not only leads
men to make wicked and perverse uses of these graces given by
God. . . .but it even leads them to use these graces not having been
given them by God. . . .

He, then, that has these supernatural gifts and graces ought to refrain from desiring to practice them, and from rejoicing in so doing, nor ought he care to exercise them; for God, Who gives Himself to such persons, by supernatural means for the profit of His Church and of its members, will move them. . .in such a manner and at such time as He desires. . . . [Ascent of Mount Carmel, *Bk. III*]

John of the Cross goes on to point out that one who is eager for spiritual powers and gifts can lose the gift of true faith, for he or she can either replace faith by miracles, and in this way "tempt God," or can build faith on "signs and wonders," and have no genuine faith at all. He adds that persons eager for spiritual powers "commonly fall into vainglory or some other vanity."

For even their joy in these wonders, when it is not. . .purely in God and for God, is vanity; which is evident in the reproof given by our Lord to the disciples when they rejoiced that the devils were subject to them; for which joy, if it had not been vain, he would not have reproved them. [Idem)

When the soul forsakes its rejoicing in divine powers and works, John continues, it magnifies and exalts both God and itself. It exalts God with the purest faith, hope and love, and "this. . .leads essentially and directly to the perfect union of the soul with God." (*Idem*]

We find the same spiritual doctrines in the Russian spiritual teachers, the erudite Bishop Theophan the Recluse in the last century, and the unlettered Staretz Silouan of Mt. Athos in our own. But let us conclude this section with an extract from the writing of a common father of Christians in both East and West, the blessed John Cassian:

Finally the Author Himself of all miracles and mighty works, when he called His disciples to learn His teaching, clearly showed what those true and specially chosen followers ought chiefly to learn from Him, saying: "Come and learn of Me," not chiefly to cast out devils by the power of heaven, not to cleanse the lepers, not to give sight to the blind, not to raise the dead: for even though I do these things by some of My servants, yet man's estate cannot insert itself into the praises of God, nor can a minister and servant gather hereby any portion for himself there where is the glory of Deity alone.

But do ye, says He, learn this of Me, "for I am meek and lowly of heart." For this it is which it is possible for all men generally to learn and practise, but the working of miracles and signs is not always necessary, nor good for all, nor granted to all.

Humility therefore is the mistress of all virtues, it is the surest foundation of the heavenly building, it is the special and splendid gift of the Saviour. For he can perform all the miracles which Christ did, without danger of being puffed up, who follow the gentle Lord not in the grandeur of His miracles, but in the virtues of patience and humility.

But he who aims at commanding unclean spirits, or bestowing gifts of healing, or showing some wonderful miracle to the people, even though when he is showing off he invokes the name of Christ, yet he is far from Christ, because in his pride of heart he does not follow his humble Teacher.

For when He was returning to the Father, He prepared, so to speak, His will and left this to His disciples: "A new commandment," said He, "give I unto you, that ye love one another; as I have loved you, so do ye also love one another:" and at once He added: "By this shall all men know that ye are My disciples, if ye have love to one another." He says not: "if ye do signs and miracles in the same way," but: "if ye have love to one another;" and this it is certain that none but the meek and humble can keep.

Wherefore our predecessors never reckoned those as good monks or free from the fault of vainglory, who professed themselves exorcists among men, and proclaimed with boastful ostentation among admiring crowds the grace which they had either obtained or which they claimed. . . .

And so if any one does any of these things in our presence, he ought to meet with commendation from us not from admiration of his miracles, but from the beauty of his life, nor should we ask whether the devils are subject to him, but whether he possesses those features of love which the Apostle describes.

And in truth it is a greater miracle to root out from one's own flesh the incentives to wantoness than to cast out unclean spirits from the bodies of others, and it is a grander sign to restrain the fierce passions of anger by the virtue of patience than to command the powers of the air, and it is a greater thing to have shut out the devouring pangs of gloominess from one's own heart than to have expelled the sickness of another and the fever of his body.

Finally it is in many ways a grander virtue and a more splendid achievement to cure the weaknesses of one's own soul than those of the body of another. For just as the soul is higher than the flesh, so is its salvation of more importance, and as its nature is more precious and excellent, so is its destruction more grievous and dangerous.

And of those cures it was said to the blessed Apostles: "Rejoice not that the devils are subject to you" For this was wrought not by their own power, but by the might of the Name invoked. And therefore they are warned not to presume to claim for themselves any blessedness or glory on this account as it was done simply by the power and might of God, but only on account of the inward purity of their life and heart, for which it was granted to them to have their names written in heaven. [Second Conference of Abbot Nesteros]

CHAPTER VI

THE SPIRIT IN THE WORLD

Some Christians claim that God's only direct action in the life of humanity, through his Son and his Spirit, takes place within God's covenant community: the people of Israel of old, and the Christian Church of the messianic era. Those who hold such a view interpret the doctrine that there is no salvation outside of Christ and his Church in an "institutional" way. With some possible exceptions for God's gracious mercy upon the "invincibly ignorant," they say, with great pathos, that a person's salvation consists in his or her conscious conversion to Jesus Christ as Lord and Savior, followed by membership in the Christian Church. Some who hold this view understand the Church as the invisible society of the elect who have been saved by faith in Christ as their "personal Savior"; others, as the visible institutional organization established and guided by Christ on earth. Both have the firm conviction that the saving grace of the Holy Spirit is found exclusively within the churchly community.

Other Christians today hold that God acts through his Son and his Spirit directly in the world; in nature, society, and history. These people see God as the author of an all-embracing plan of salvation worked out within the processes of history, culminating in the final establishment of the Kingdom of God. Those who lean toward this second general perspective understand the primary task of the Christian Church and its members as locating how and where God is acting in the world, in nature and history, in society and politics, by the power of his Spirit, and then to get involved in these divinely inspired processes and to cooperate with God's Spirit in them for the sake of human salvation.

The first general view defends a Christian and churchly maximalism, if not a strictly sectarian Christian ecclesiastical exclusivism, in regard to salvation. The second is extremely minimalistic, if not radically relativistic, about the place of Christ and the Church in a person's spiritual life and ultimate destiny. We might, in addition, "symbolize" each view generally with a reference to the significance of Christian mission. The first approach would understand Christian mission primarily as the conversion of sinners to faith in Jesus Christ as Lord and Savior, with subsequent membership in the Christian Church considered essential for salvation—whether the "church" is understood as an invisible fellowship of believers, or a visible institutional organization on earth. The second approach would understand Christian mission primarily, as the involvement of the Church and its members in the social, political, and historical processes of the world—both "secular" and "religious"—through which the Spirit of God, known by Christians in Jesus, is seen to be saving humanity by building the Kingdom of God in history.

The proponents of these fundamentally opposing views are sometimes—unfortunately and misleadingly—labeled "conservative" and "liberal"; or "evangelical" and "social"; or "traditionalist" and "modernist"; or "religious" and "secular." The members of each group can quote the Scriptures to their own advantage, an ability which was once quite rightly ascribed to the devil. They are also able to quote the fathers and the saints of the church to suit their positions.

The question now is whether or not these mutually opposed views are proper in the first place and are adequate to the facts of divine revelation in Christ and the Spirit. Must one accept the fundamental opposition, or do we not have, once again, a tragically hopeless situation arising out of a misplacing of the questions in the first place? I believe that this latter is exactly the case, and will try to show from the perspective of the Orthodox Church, as I understand it, how this is so.

First, I believe that we must liberate ourselves from positing a fundamental opposition between God acting in the Church and God acting in the world, understood as God's good creation, as if these two actions were independent and mutually exclusive. The New Testament Scriptures may tend to lead some into such an understanding by using the terms "the world" and "the flesh" as expressions for sinful and graceless existence in radical opposition to the life of the Kingdom of God, the life of grace in God's Spirit. But we have to be very careful on this point. For indeed it is true that we find such expressions in the Scriptures, for example, in the Gospel according to St. John:

"If you love me, you will keep my commandments. And I will pray the Father, and he will give you another Counselor, to be with you for ever, even the Spirit of truth, whom the world cannot receive, because it neither sees him nor knows him. . . ." [John 14:15-17]

"If the world hates you, know that it has hated me before it hated you. If you were of the world, the world would love its own; but because you are not of the world, but I chose you out of the world, therefore the world hates you." [John 15:18-19]

Do not love the world or the things in the world. If any one loves the world, love for the Father is not in him. For all that is in the world, the lust of the flesh and the lust of the eyes and the pride of life, is not of the Father but is of the world. And the world passes away, and the lust of it; but he who does the will of God abides for ever. [1 John 2:15-18, cf. 1 Corinthians 7:31]

If such were the only texts of the Scriptures we had, we would of course be very tempted to consider "the world" as radically worthless and devoid of God's grace. But we have other words, for example in the same writings of St. John, to keep us from yielding totally to this view.

He was in the world, and the world was made through him, yet the world knew him not. [John 1:10]

For God so loved the world that he gave his only Son, that whoever believes in him should not perish but have eternal life. For God sent the Son into the world, not to condemn the world, but that the world might be saved. . . .[John 3:16-17]

We discover the same ambiguous meaning given to the term "the flesh" in the Scriptures. Already, we have seen how St. Paul insisted on the opposition between "the flesh" and "the Spirit" in his letter to the Romans.

For those who live according to the flesh set their minds on the things of the flesh, but those who live according to the Spirit set their minds on the things of the Spirit. To set the mind on the flesh is death, but to set the mind on the Spirit is life and peace. For the mind that is set on the flesh is hostile to God; it does not submit to God's law, indeed it cannot; and those who are in the flesh cannot please God. But you are not in the flesh, you are in the Spirit, if the Spirit of God really dwells in you. . . .[Romans 8:5-9]

It is clear, however, that for St. Paul "the flesh" does not mean God's creation itself, for in this same letter, indeed in the same chapter, he writes about creation in the following way:

For the creation waits with eager longing for the revealing of the sons of God; for the creation was subjected to futility, not of its own will but by the will of him who subjected it in hope; because the creation itself will be set free from its bondage to decay and obtain the glorious liberty of the children of God. We know that the whole creation has been groaning in travail together until now; and not the creation, but we ourselves, who have the first fruits of the Spirit, groan inwardly as we wait for adoption as sons, the redemption of our bodies. [Romans 8:19-23]

In other New Testament texts, the term "flesh" does not have the negative connotation given to it by the apostle Paul when used as the catchword for humankind's sinfully carnal existence devoid of God's Spirit. For example, in St. John we find the following passages:

And the Word became flesh, and dwelt among us, full of grace and truth; we beheld his glory, glory as of the only begotten Son of the Father. . . .And from his fulness have we all received, grace upon grace. [John 1:14-16]

By this you know the Spirit of God: every spirit which confesses that Jesus Christ has come in the flesh is of God, and every spirit which does not confess Jesus is not of God. [1 John 4:2-3]

And in the last days it shall be, God declares, that I will pour out my Spirit on all flesh. . . .moreover my flesh will dwell in hope. For Thou will not abandon my soul to Hades [i.e. Death], nor let thy Holy One see corruption. . . .[Acts 2:17, 26; Cf. Joel 2:28-32, Psalm16:8-11]

Concerning the terms "the world and "the flesh," therefore, we must make the following conclusions. As creations of God, the world and the flesh are good. The Word of God himself "becomes flesh" in order to save "the world" by the indwelling of his Spirit. But as terms describing God's good creation in rebellion against God, devoid of God's Spirit, these same terms are symbolic of Spiritless, graceless existence. On this point, we can refer to the writings of the saints. First, St. John Chrysostom:

"And the world knew Him not." [John 1:10] By "the world" here is meant the multitude which is corrupt and closely fused with earthly things, the vulgar, turbulent, silly people. For the friends and favorites of God all knew Him, even before His coming in the flesh.

"The world," he says, "knew Him not;" but they "of whom the world was not worthy" [cf. Hebrews 11:38] knew Him. And having spoken of those who knew Him not, he in a short time puts the cause of their ignorance. . .that is, those persons who are as it were nailed to the world alone, and who mind only the things of the world. For

so was Christ Himself minded to call them when he says, "Holy Father, the world hath not known Thee." [John 17:25]

For Scripture is accustomed to call by the name "the world" both the creation, and those who live in wickedness. . . . And these things it is necessary to know exactly that we may not, through the signification of words, offer a handle to the heretics. [Homilies on St. John, 8 and 66]

And also John Cassian.

We find that the word "flesh" is used in holy scriptures with many different meanings: for sometimes it stands for the whole man. . . . Sometimes it stands for carnal and sinful man. . . . Sometimes it is used for sins themselves. . . . Sometimes it stands for blood relationship. . . . We must therefore inquire in which of these four meanings we ought to take the word "flesh. . . ."

Wherefore in this passage ["The flesh lusteth against the Spirit"] *we ought to take "flesh" as meaning not man. . . . but the carnal will and evil desires. . . .* (Conference of Abbot Daniel, 10,11)

And St. Isaac of Syria.

When you [monks] *hear that it is necessary to withdraw from the world, to leave the world, to purify yourself from all that belongs to the world, you must first learn and understand the term "world" not in its normal everyday use, but in its purely interior meaning. . . .*

"World" is a collective name [in this sense] *embracing what are called* [sinful] *passions. When we want to speak of passions collectively we call them "the world." When we want to distinguish them by their different names, we call them passions.*

"The world" [in this sense] *is carnal life and the minding of the flesh. Therefore a person is seen to be liberated from "the world" inasmuch as he has been liberated from this.*

*Passions are something added to the soul through the fault of the
soul itself. . . . the nature of the soul was luminous and pure
through participation in the Divine Light. . . the soul abandons its
proper nature when it is moved by passions, as the children of the
Church assert.* [*Directions on Spiritual Training*]

St. Gregory Palamas even claims that a human being's body and
his or her being in the world as its master actually make human
beings superior to the angels, who do not have this vocation from
God. He writes that the Word became flesh "in order to honor the
flesh, even this mortal flesh. . . for apart from sin, nothing is wrong
in itself in the present life. . . ." (Homily 16)

*In the same way the Divinity of the Word Incarnate is common to
both the soul and the body. . . so the grace of the Spirit in spiritual
men is transmitted to the body by the soul. . . and this gives the
body the experience of the divine. . . then the body is no longer
driven by bodily and material passions. . . but. . . rejects all
relation with evil and is inspired for its own sanctification and
inalienable deification. . . .*

*Clearly we have been ordered to "crucify the flesh with its passions
and desires"* [*Galatians 5:24*]*. . . we have not been told this in order
to kill ourselves by killing the activity of the body and all powers of
the soul. . . .* [*Second Triad*]

The monks Kallistos and Ignatios summed up this attitude to the
body when they wrote that "the fathers have taught us to be killers of
the passions and not killers of the body." (*Directions to Hesychasts*)
Even in this stringently ascetic view, therefore, there is no division
between the spirit as good and the body as evil. Passions are not
synonymous with sin, certainly not with the body, or with the flesh
or the world as such. There are evil passions, "vile" and
"blameworthy" passions (to quote St. Maximus), which are both of
the soul and of the body. Being evil, such passions as are sometimes,
called in the Scriptures, symbolically and collectively, "the flesh"
and "the world." However, as St. John Chrysostom has specifically

warned us, let us be careful not to give "a handle to the heretics" who would gladly confuse God's good creation with human evil and the perverse use of it through the sinful passions rooted, as St. Maximus has said, in "self-love," which considers the body, the flesh, and the world as ends in themselves.

It remains for us to attempt to articulate the relationship between "the Church which is his (Christ's) Body, the fulness of him who fills all in all" (Ephesians 1:23) and "the world" understood as the ongoing life of man's history and activity in space and time.

The "image" in which all humans are made is Christ, and the Church of Christ, not identical with or limited to its human members, but as "the life of the Spirit in humanity" (Fr. Bulgakov) and the "body of Christ" (St. Paul), is itself the "recreation of the world." (St. Gregory of Nyssa) Therefore, what humankind is and the world is—or rather what humankind must be and the world must be—is revealed, and given as a gift to man and the world, in Christ and the Church. In Christ and the Church there is "newness of life." "All things" in them "are made new." There is a "new man" and a "new creation," a "new heaven" and "new earth." There is in this "newness" a "fulness" as well: the "fulness of grace and truth," the "fulness of life," the "fulness of divinity bodily," the "fulness of God," the "fulness of him Who fill all in all." It is from the perspective of *newness* and *fulness* that the old, partial, fragmented, sinful world, which is "missing the mark" in regard to its true nature and purpose, is to be seen and appreciated by Christians. Christ came "not to condemn the world but that the world through him might be saved" (John 3:17), "not to destroy men's lives, but to save them." The salvation of human life and the life of the world is given in the newness and fulness of Christ and the Church.

Once more, we must consider what salvation means. Salvation simply means genuine life. It is the knowledge of the truth in the proper vision (*theoreia*) and action(*praxis*) of life. It does not happen or begin "after we die." It is genuine life, eternal life, divine life, life in abundance, life in the truth and love of God, begun already now within the conditions of life in this world, by the indwelling of God's Spirit in men and women, fully given in Christ and the Church. It is the life of growth in divine perfection, to "the measure of the stature of the fulness of Christ," given to human beings so that, as "partakers of the divine nature," human persons may be and become that for which they are created by God. Salvation is the life of God himself which all who are saved will live in God's unending Kingdom at the close of the ages, through his Son and his Spirit.

Salvation also cannot be pronounced or imputed to human persons "from outside." It cannot be the act of God alone, arbitrarily forced upon creatures. Human persons must be open to salvation. They must be "competent" of salvation in the freedom of their own minds and hearts. They must "choose life" by the grace of God's Spirit, in the full and sovereign integrity of their own persons which the Spirit gives. God can save no one against his will because salvation is the voluntary conformity, by the indwelling of God's Spirit, of the human will with God's. For this reason, salvation is always *personal*—not *individual*, but *personal*. It requires the living action of human *persons*, by grace, in union with the action of God, so that God's action and human action become one theandric action, one co-action of the divine and the human, without separation or division and without fusion or mixture between what is of God and what is human.

Wherever and however a person does good, knows the truth, creates beauty, edifies creation, he or she does so by God's Spirit, and to this extent he or she is "saved." However "brutalized" or "demonized" human beings may be, by their own free choice or by the captivity and enslavement of their minds and hearts to evil, by the "culture of evil" called the "sin of the world" into which they are born and in which they live, the image of God in them yet still remains. It may be deformed and perverted, covered by filth and corrupted, but still it remains.

For salvation to occur, for a man to live the life of God, his nature must be purified and restored. This happens always, however it takes place, by God's Word and Spirit—the Word and the Spirit given to all human beings by nature in creation, revealed in the Law and the prophets, who come in their own persons in the final and everlasting covenant of the Kingdom of God in the Church.

If a person, not having heard of the Law and the prophets, or of Christ and the Holy Spirit in the Church, lives "according of nature," that is, according to the Word and the Spirit of God as given in creation, he will be "saved" by the will and the action of God. Although such a person may not consciously be aware ot it, he or she is in communion with God, through the Word and the Spirit, to the extent that he or she lives in goodness, in truth, and in love. On this point, St. Paul is clear.

For he will render to every man according to his works: to those who by patience in well-doing seek for glory and honor and immortality, he will give eternal life; but for those who are factious and do not obey the truth, but obey wickedness, there will be wrath and fury. There will be tribulation and distress for every human being who does evil, the Jew first and also the Greek, but glory and honor and peace for every one who does good, the Jew first and also the Greek. For God shows no partiality.

All who have sinned without the law will also perish without the law, and all who have sinned under the law will be judged by the law. For it is not the hearers of the law who are righteous before God, but the doers of the law who will be justified. When Gentiles who have not the law do by nature what the law requires, they are a law to themselves, even though they do not have the law. They show that what the law requires is written on their hearts, while their conscience also bears witness and their conflicting thoughts accuse or perhaps excuse them on that day when, according to my gospel, God judges the secrets of men by Christ Jesus. [Romans 2:6-16]

The point here is that when persons have no access to God's manifestation in the dispensation of salvation in Israel and the Church, or when the dispensation itself is perverted and obscured by those who claim to believe it and live by it, and when people do what God requires of human beings as well as they can through their God-given, God-imaged, and God-inspired humanity, they are pleasing in God's sight, and God himself will guide them as well as he can within the available conditions and possibilities of human freedom and life. This is the meaning of divine providence.

God cannot and does not force himself on his creatures. He does not force himself even on Israel. He chose Israel because in that nation he knew—or "foreknew" or "knows"—that there would be people competent and capable of being filled with grace to hear God's Word and to cooperate with his Spirit. This dispensation of salvation in Israel and the Church is not an arbitrary favor of God, a capricious and whimsical choice of the Almighty. It is, we might say, the choice that God had to make if, by his grace, he were going to act to save his creation, or even to create in the first place. Simply put, God has to work with what he has. He chooses "what is foolish in the world. . . what is weak. . . ." (1 Corinthians 1:27) But his choice and his action would still be without effect and without result, if these foolish and weak were not in some way willing and able to "shame the wise and strong in the world." For this reason, Abraham and Moses, Mary and John the Baptist, the prophets and the apostles, the martyrs and the saints are worthy of praise. For this reason, believers honor them as those "of whom the world was not worthy." (Hebrews 11:38) For this reason, all generations call them "blessed." (Cf. Luke 1:48) For this reason, they were chosen by God, not because of their "works" but because of their willingness to work with the grace of God, their ability to be the "earthen vessels" through whom it is clearly revealed that "the transcendent power belongs to God" alone. (Cf. 2 Corinthians 4:7)

We see this clearly in the "repentant persecutor" Paul, not to mention the hesitant Moses and the unwilling Jeremiah. Paul was converted because he was willing and able to be converted. It took some divinely dramatic action to do the trick, but the action itself was undertaken by God, who knows what he is doing and how it has to be done, because God knew that something of a violent character was required to change the violent character of the zealous persecutor Saul into the zealous apostle Paul. (Cf. Acts 7-9) This also, in a similar way, is the case of Mary the Virgin.

It is a dogma of the Orthodox Church that God's Son could not have been born from just anyone; God could not merely "choose a womb" for the incarnation of his Son. Mary had to be personally competent to be the Theotokos: the one who gives birth to God in the flesh, the bearer of Immanuel. Mary had to be "produced" and "cultivated" within the People of God. She had to be formed spiritually by her inspired progenitors. She had to be one "full of grace" and "blessed among women." She had to be made personally willing and worthy to be the mother of the divine Messiah.

The Son of God was not born from a *body*. He was born from a *person*, the human person made capable by grace to be the "living temple" of him whom "the heavens cannot contain." Such are the expressions of Orthodox hymnology for the feasts of the Virgin Mother, as well as for those of the Annunciation and Nativity of Christ. We can take as example of this the *kontakion* of the feast of the entrance of the child Mary to the Jerusalem temple:

The most pure temple of the Savior,
The precious chamber and virgin,
The sacred treasury of the glory of God,
Is presented today to the house of the Lord.
She brings with her the grace of the Spirit,
Which the angels of God do praise:
Truly this woman is the Abode of Heaven.

And the hymn to the Theotokos from the eucharistic liturgy of St. Basil the Great:

All of creation rejoices in You,
O Full of Grace,
The assembly of angels and the human race.
O Consecrated Temple.
O Spiritual Paradise.
The Glory of Virgins,
From Whom God was incarnate
And became a little child,
Our God before the ages.
He made your body His throne,
And your womb more spacious than the heavens.
All of creation rejoices in you,
O Full of grace; glory to you!

Thus we have the church fathers from the second century calling Mary the "new Eve" who becomes the true "mother of the living" because of her personal obedience and voluntary cooperation with the Spirit of God—the one who "hears the Word of God and keeps it." (Luke 11:28; St. Justin Martyr, St. Irenaeus, et al.) And we have as well the liturgy of the Church, with the fathers giving symbolically to Mary all of the images of the Old Testament theophanies of the glory and presence of God with man: Jacob's ladder, the burning bush, the mountain of Sinai, the Jerusalem Temple. And we find the Church as well giving its full and unhesitating corroboration to the bold doctrine which claims that: All men are indebted to God for their salvation; and God Himself is indebted to Mary. For without the "let it be" of Mary, inspired by grace and filled with God's Spirit, the Savior could not have come.

If we forget the radical necessity of human freedom in cooperation with divine grace, the freedom which is enabled by divine grace, we are certain to fall into absurd and impossible questions and answers. And this, I believe, is exactly what has happened. The Christian faith, and "religion" itself, is looked upon by all too many as being virtually the exclusive activity of God without reference to man's freedom and his personal and cultural integrity and reality; a reality closed up in itself without direct reference to, and often in radical opposition to, the life of the direct reference to, and often in radical opposition to, the life of the world which God so loves and for which Christ, his divine Son, has died. The Christian faith is looked upon as merely a "means of salvation" for "another life" beyond and in opposition to the life of the world in which we now live. It is looked upon as a thing-in-itself, a locked-up system of doctrines and practices radically opposed to the doctrines and practices of "secular man"—if it is not then, on the contrary, simply "secularized" itself. With such an understanding and approach, it is inevitable that impossible questions should arise:

Can you get saved outside the church, or do you have to be in it?—the implication being, of course, that if you don't "have" to be in it, why be in it?

What do you have to do to be saved?—the implication being: Would you please set out the minimum requirements of what a person "has to do" to be "saved."

Do you have to believe only? Or do you also have to do good? Do you have to go to church? Or can you be saved by praying at home? Do you have to have sacraments? Or can you get along with some other "means of grace"? Is the Bible sufficient? Or do you need other sources of information? If so, what sources? If not, why not? And what about the good Buddhist? Or the honest atheist? Or the sacrificial humanist? Not to mention unbaptized babies. Will they go to heaven? Can they? Or will God send them to hell because they are not baptized Christians? And if they can go to heaven, then why be a Christian? And if they cannot is God really just? Is he really love? Does he really rule the world? And how about the celebrated African bushman who has never heard of Jesus? What about his eternal destiny? And what about the baptized church members who don't really believe? And what about those who claim to believe, but to continue to sin?

All these questions, which really bother people—virtually every religious discussion comes around to them almost at once—are born of a low and unworthy view of man, life, religion, the Church, and God himself. It is a "consumer" view, in which one wants to get the most by doing the least. One does not want to grow in the truth that makes men free *right here and now*, but only to be "certain" and "secure" with the least possible effort and action. One wants not to seek, to knock, to find, to grow, to confront life with the ultimate questions and to face reality honestly and openly, on the basis of one's own understanding and experience of things and the spiritual testimony of others. Such as attitude is low and unworthy because with it no one can "be saved and come to the knowledge of the truth" (Cf. 1 Timothy 2:4), because he is not interested in the truth. He is merely interested in arranging things in the most painless and comfortable way possible, with the greatest security and the least tension and effort in spiritual conflict with oneself, with others, with the world, and with God.

The reduction of religion to the issue of "salvation" understood as "going to heaven" on the basis of some inscrutable will of God with the least possible effort, is a destructive and corruptive perversion of religion and life. It reduces a person's spiritual life to the level of obscene and prurient spiritual interests. It reduces a person's quest for spiritual satisfaction and security to the lowest level. It reduces God himself—and his Son, his Spirit and his Church—to a mere "means" of attaining a desired "end."

According to the catholic tradition of the church, the decision and the knowledge of who is "going to heaven" is left to God alone. It is his business, after all. He alone knows the minds and hearts of his creatures. He alone knows what they do with the measure of faith, freedom, and grace given to them. It is impossible for human beings to know and judge. For, as St. Isaac of Syria said, even to know *oneself* as one really is is a greater feat than raising the dead—not to speak about knowing *others*. And John of the Cross has taught that the interest to know who is saved, even oneself, is of no profit anyway. It is a waste of time, effort, and energy to pursue it. It is the succumbing to temptation because, first of all, the possibility to reach sound conclusions are almost impossible; even if one should come to see the truth about oneself or another, life must go on in continual effort facing the continual possibility of falling away. Thus, it is wisdom itself not to be bothered about "who is saved"—even oneself—but just to strive constantly to love God and neighbor in fidelity to Christ in every word, deed and thought, in each smallest thing, in every actual moment.

This is the approach to the spiritual life in the teaching of the saints. One must strive only to be faithful to God, to oneself, to others, to the Church, to the truth, to life itself. And what God does is his business. We know that it will be proper and just, whatever it is, and we need not fret about it. This is exactly what is taught in the Scriptures. When the Lord comes to judge his people, he should find them watching and working, and not debating about whom he is saving. Christ has said that "to whom much is given, of him will much be required." (Luke 12:48) There is, therefore, no moment of certitude when one can say that he—or anyone—has done with his life that which God has required on the basis of what God has given. Only God knows. And whether we know or not makes absolutely no difference about what we should be and do. Our very desire to know is a sin. It is foolishness. It is the yielding to a prurient interest without redeeming value, eternal or otherwise.

No one was more certain of his salvation in Christ that St. Paul. And yet he persisted in his efforts of faithful service and love lest he who preached to others might himself "be disqualified." (1 Corinthians 9:27) When St. Paul ordered the sinful Corinthian to be removed from the church community, he did so not to judge him or damn him to hell, but, while others were being spared his evil influence within the body, he himself might perhaps be "saved in the day of the Lord" because of his exclusion. (1 Corinthians 5:5) St. Paul is clear on this point—we are obliged to follow his teaching:

For what have I to do with judging outsiders? Is it not those inside the church whom you are to judge? God judges those outside. "Drive out the wicked person from among you." [1 Corinthians 5:12-13]

I do not even judge myself, but I am not thereby acquitted. It is the Lord who judges me. Therefore do not pronounce judgment before the time, before the Lord comes, who will bring to light the things now hidden in darkness and will disclose the purposes of the heart. Then every man will receive his commendation from God. [1 Corinthians 4:3-5]

Christians, therefore, should continue to serve God and human beings in truth and love, in every smallest detail, being absolutely certain that their salvation is in Christ and the Spirit of God, hoping that they are actually doing what the Lord requires on the basis of what they have been given. Christians should strive only to do the truth, to bear fruit, to multiple their talents that they might hear the words of the Lord: "Well done, good and faithful servant. . . enter into the joy of your master." (Matthew 25:24) This should be the Christian's only interest and desire, only passionate intention: to please the Lord and to leave the rest up to him. We see this point made sharply in the lives of the saints who refused to place judgment on others, and refused to be presumptuous about their own eternal destiny.

Having insisted on this point, we must still consider the action of

God's Spirit outside the membership of the community of the Church.

First, we could not even put the question if we did not have the knowledge and experience of the Holy Spirit within the Church. We receive the Spirit and know the Spirit as members of the Body of Christ. Within the body, we know who the Spirit of God is, what he is like, and how he acts. Through the Spirit, we know that Jesus is the Christ, and that the Christ is the Lord. We know that Jesus Christ is the eternal and uncreated Son and Word of God, the Creator of heaven and earth and all things visible and invisible who became man for the salvation of all men and the whole of creation. We know that without him, and without his Church, there can be no salvation for man and his world. We know that he brings and gives the Kingdom of God to man as a gift, the gift bought by his own blood on the cross. We know all this because he has given us of his own Spirit, the Spirit who is the eternal, divine, uncreated Spirit of God, the Spirit of Truth who guides us unto all truth and teaches us about everything, the Spirit of Christ who is the pledge and the guarantee, the very presence in our lives of the Kingdom of God.

Knowing all this in the Spirit, we share in the newness and fulness of God. We are new people who share in the new life of the new creation, in the new heaven and new earth. We partake of God's fulness in Christ, the fulness of life, the fulness of truth and "grace upon grace." We are temples of the Holy Spirit and members of Christ's body, the Church, the "fulness of him who fills all in all." (Ephesians 1:23) We belong to the Church of the living God, "the pillar and bulwark of truth" (1 Timothy 3:15)

As members of the Church, we are purified and enlightened by faith and by grace—not by works of the law, lest any man should boast. We know what is the height and the depth and the breadth and the width. We know what is going on and what life is all about. We know the source of our being and the purpose of our existence. We know the mystery of God's plan from before the ages, hidden from the angels and made known in the Church. We know, in other words, what salvation is, and what it means to be saved. We know what man must be and must do to be in everlasting communion with God. But because "the heart is deceitful above all things and is desperately corrupt" (Jeremiah 17:9), and because it is utter foolishness to "rely on your own insight" and to be "wise in your own eyes," (Proverbs 3:5, 7) we know that it is wisdom itself not to judge others, lest we be judged and condemned ourselves by God, particularly for not producing the fruits of the Spirit in our lives according to measure of grace and talents given to us. So we make no claims about our own eternal salvation, or that of others, but merely strive for righteousness in our lives according to the ways shown to us by God through Christ, his Word incarnate, and his most Holy Spirit in the Church.

In our striving for righteousness according to the truth that is in Jesus, we strive in faith to "discern the spirits" everywhere (1 Corinthians 12:10), to try them, to "see whether they are of God." (1 John 4:1) We can recognize the action of the spirits that are inspired by the Spirit of God, by their fruits: love, joy, peace, patience, kindness, goodness, faithfulness, gentleness, self-control. (Galatians 5:22) We pray not to be deceived by the vain imaginations of our minds and hearts, and still more, not to be the deceivers of others. (Cf. Job 12:16, 2 Timothy 3:13) But we go on in faith, refusing judgment in personal cases, including our own, while discerning and testing the words and actions of all, to see if they are of God, inspired by his Spirit, in conformity with his Son Jesus. We do this strictly on the basis of God's self-revelation and action in the Church, in his Son and his Spirit, in his scriptures, sacraments, and saints. For here, we believe, is the clear manifestation and gift of the newness and the fulness of the Kingdom of God who cannot and does not deceive. Here is the sole criterion for our discernment, our vision and our action. Here, is our whole life, the life that we wish all men to share with us because we know that it comes from God and is God's.

Knowing this and having this experience, we know that all human beings are God's, made in his image and according to his likeness. We know that the world is his, the work of his hands and the object of his unwavering love. We know that he has created all creation for himself, and that it will be restless and in agony, groaning and in travail, until it comes to perfection and fulness of life in him—a perfection always to become more complete. And we know that wherever and in whomever there is anything good and beautiful and true, it is only because he is there, with his Word, in his Spirit, allowing it and making it this way.

Thus, we follow the apostle Paul in his teaching, which we believe and know by our own personal experience to be of God. We think about, seek, desire, and affirm "whatever is true, whatever is honorable, whatever is just, whatever is pure, whatever is lovely, whatever is gracious, if there is any excellence, if there is anything worthy of praise. . . " (Philippians 4:8). We do so, we hope, wherever these fruits of the action of God's Spirit appear in truth: in Christians or in non-Christians, in believers or in nonbelievers, within the membership of the Church of God or outside it.

Discerning the spirits of men, and testing them, we see that God's Spirit is actually present and active in many who are not in the household of faith or in the Church. We can see their fruits, however, because we believe that we are, by God's grace and mercy in Christ, within the light of his truth and love in the Church. We do not know why people who manifest the fruits of the Spirit are not in the Church. And we do not pass judgment about their ultimate destiny with God. Perhaps they have not had a clear and adequate chance of knowing the Lord Jesus Christ, or perhaps they fail to see that God is in Christ because of the weaknesses and sins of the Christians. For it will certainly be to our condemnation, to whom so much has been given, if the Lord's terrible words are directed at us: "The name of God is blasphemed among the nations because of you." (Romans 2:24, cf. Isaiah 52:5)

Can there be any doubt that there are at least some, if not many, among the nations who reject the name of God and his Christ because of us sinners who call on his name and honor him with our lips but are far from his presence in our lives and deeds? Can there by any doubt that there are at least some whose lives are lived according to the image of God in whom they are made, and by the grace of God's Spirit by whom they are inspired, who will receive the mercy of God for life everlasting, while we ourselves who have preached and prophesied, and have done many mighty works, will be lost?

The fact that we can say this does not mean that the Church is not essential to human life; that it is not true, complete, perfect, full, the only way of human salvation. It means rather that the way of the

Church, the way of Christ, may be followed by those who, for reasons known to God alone, are not members of Christ's Church on earth, but are somehow united to his Church because they live by his Spirit. We could say, and we must say theoretically, that such persons, given the opportunity, freely and clearly, to see and to choose, would choose God and life and become disciples of Christ and members of the church. It is the Christians' mission to offer the chance: to speak the words of truth and to do them in our lives. If we fail to do this, it in no way alters the fact that Christ is the Truth, the Holy Spirit is the Spirit of Truth, and the Church, with its Scriptures, sacraments, and saints, is the pillar and bulwark of truth. Our failure to do this only insures our condemnation. And about the salvation of those outside—as St. Paul has said—that is up to God.

With this view we can in no way conclude, however, that there is some kind of cosmic, historical process going on, directed by God, for the salvation of mankind. In the first place, it must be soundly denied that the Spirit of God acts otherwise in history than in and through human persons. There are no "spiritual powers" which are not personal, no actions of God's Spirit in history which are not done through humans created in the image and likeness of God, who is Christ. And also there are no "evil powers" which can act in human beings without their consent and cooperation. What happens to the world in human history is solely and exclusively dependent upon humanity. Where men and women cooperate with God and are inspired by God's Spirit; where they love, do good, build up, create beauty, live in truth, then God's will is done and his Kingdom comes. Where human persons are evil, cooperating with the deceiver, adversary, and enemy of man, the devil, then there is hell: corruption, perversion, falsehood, destruction, and death. In the traditional Christian view, human history is a drama, a warfare, a struggle. There is a cosmic battle going on between the children of light and the children of darkness—and we must be bold enough to say that there are children of light who are not formal members of the Church, and children of darkness who are: the heretics, false prophets, false brethren, blind guides; those who "tamper with God's word" (2 Corinthians 4:2); who "twist (the Scriptures) to their own destruction" (2 Peter 3:16); who hold "the form of religion" but deny "its power" (2 Timothy 3:5); who "have a zeal for God, but it is not enlightened" (Romans 10:2); who, in a word, fall under the condemnation of Christ Who said that they "shut the kingdom of heaven against men" for they "neither enter themselves nor allow those who would enter to go in" for they "traverse land and sea to make one convert, and when he becomes a convert" they "make him twice as much a child of hell" as they are themselves. (Cf. Matthew 23:13-16) And who can doubt that this is so among Christians, and even Christian denominations and communities whose teachings and actions prevent many from entering into the fulness of life in Christ and his Church?

The cosmic drama goes on until the end of the ages. The struggle continues until the final end. Only then, when Christ comes in his glory, are the good fish kept and the rotten fish discarded. Only then is the good wheat kept and the worthless weeds burned. Only then is the judgment, the *krisis* (which means "separation") between the sheep and the goats, those who are truly God's and those who are not. Until then the battle goes on. The true Christians know what the result will be. They know the judge and the criterion of judgment. They know what will happen when the deeds of every man will be revealed, when Christ comes to lay bare the hearts of men and to judge each one according to his works. (Cf. Matthew 16:27, Revelation 2:23) They know this because in Christ it is all already fulfilled. The end of the ages has come. The Messiah has appeared. The Holy Spirit has been given. There is nothing still to be made known. Christ has been crucified, and history has reached its term. Christ has been glorified and the Kingdom has been revealed. The Spirit has been given and we live in the last time. Who knows how long this "last time" will be? Who knows how many more persons must yet live and die before the Day of the Lord comes in power? Who knows how many more ages must yet come and go before the end of the ages will come when the dead shall rise: "those who have done good, to the resurrection of life, and those who have done evil, to the resurrection of damnation." (John 5:29) Jesus himself, in his humanity, claimed ignorance of this fact. (Matthew 24:36) And to be curious about it is another of the "prurient interests" with which only the foolish and unworthy are concerned. The task at hand is rather to fight the good fight and so to be with the children of light when the Lord's Day comes.

With this view, Christians have every right to be optimistic about the destiny of creation, for the teaching of the Lord is clear and firm. The righteous will be saved. The poor will be exalted. The meek will inherit the earth. The oppressed will receive justice. The lion and lamb will dwell together in harmony. The desert will blossom with flowers in abundance. Water springs will gush forth in the wilderness. Every valley will be exalted, every mountain and hill made plain, the crooked—straight, the rough edges—plain. And all flesh will behold the glory of God in the face of Christ, for he will be all, and in all, through his Spirit.

What we do in history, therefore, is critical. What we do with our world is of eternal significance. History has a meaning and goal—not in itself, for history as such, or some spirit of history, does not exist. There is only the activity of human persons with and within the creation of God. Nothing of value will be lost. The smallest goodness of man, his smallest achievement, will remain forever in God, saved in Christ; indeed saved as a "element" of Christ, the whole Christ, *Totus Christus*, Head and Body. For deified humanity in the deified world will comprise the deified Body of Christ: one mind, one flesh, one soul, one body, one being, one life with Christ in God. And this comes from God's Spirit who dwells in human beings, making them "gods by grace."

Thus the destiny of creation is inextricably bound up with the destiny of humankind. For the whole of creation "waits with eager longing for the revealing of the sons of God" for then "the creation itself will be set free from its bondage to decay and obtain the glorious liberty of the children of God." (Cf. Romans 8:19-20) This is the end of human history, its term and its goal. We know this right now in the Spirit in the Church. And we long for it, we work for it, we pray for it continually: "Come Lord Jesus; yea, come quickly!"

We know this in the Church, and we want all people to know it. We experience this in the Church, and we want all people to experience it. We want all people to be in the Church of Jesus Christ right now only for this reason. For "God our Savior. . . desires all men to be saved and to come to the knowledge of the truth." (1

Timothy 2 : 4) And the Church itself is *salvation*: the fulness of Gods Kingdom, in Christ and the Spirit, in symbol and mystery, in the midst of the earth. Being in the Church we know this. And we know as well that whoever and whatever is of God in the world can never be lost. For God has acted in Christ to save all who are with him and all that is his—whether human beings know it or not—and this very salvation is the life of the saved and the judgment of those who are perishing. The Spirit of God has revealed this to us in the Church. Saint Irenaeus said it long ago: "Where the Spirit of God is there is the Church, and where the Church is, there is the Spirit of God and the fulness of grace'.(*Against Heresies*) And this too is the testimony of the elder Silouan who, when asked about the salvation of those not in the Orthodox Church, replied: "I do not know about that. But I believe only in the Orthodox Church. In her is the joy of salvation through Christ-like humility." (*Wisdom from Mount Athos*) With the world of Father Silouan we conclude our meditation on the Spirit of God.

The merciful Lord gave the Holy Spirit on earth, and by the Holy Spirit was the Holy Church established.

No man of himself can know what is Gods love, unless he be taught by the Holy Spirit; but Gods love is known in our Church through the Holy Spirit, and so we speak of His love.

It is given to our Orthodox Church through the Holy Spirit to understand the mysteries of God, and she is strong in the holiness of her thought and patience.

In heaven all things live and move by the Holy Spirit. But the same Spirit is on earth too. The Holy Spirit lives in our Church in the sacraments; in the Holy Scriptures; in the hearts of the faithful. The Holy Spirit unites all men; and so the saints are close to us; and when we pray to them they hear our prayers in the Holy Spirit, and our souls feel that they are praying for us.

How happy and blessed are we Orthodox Christians, that the Lord has given us life in the Holy Spirit. . .

Blessed are we Orthodox Christians in that the Lord loves us dearly and accords us the grace of the Holy Spirit, and in the Holy Spirit gives us to see His glory. But to preserve grace we must love our enemies and offer thanks to God for all our afflictions.

Blessed are we, Orthodox Christians, because we live under the protection of God's mercy. It is not difficult for us to wage this war: the Lord has pity on us and gave us the Holy Spirit who abides in our Church. Our only sorrow is that not everyone knows God and how greatly He loves us. The man who prays is conscious of this love, and the Spirit of God bears witness in his soul to salvation.

When the soul is full of love of God, out of the infinity of her joy she sorrows and prays in tears for the whole world that all people may come to know their Lord and heavenly Father. There is no rest for her, nor does she desire rest, until all mankind delights in the grace of His love.

O merciful Lord, give Thy grace to all the peoples of the earth that they may know Thee, for without Thy Holy Spirit man cannot know Thee and conceive Thy love.

O Lord, send down Thy mercy on the children of the earth whom Thus dost love, and give them to know Thee by the Holy Spirit.

O Lord grant all the people of the earth to know how greatly Thou lovest us, and to know the wondrous life Thou dost prepare for them that believe in Thee.

With tears I implore Thee: Hear my prayer for Thy children, and grant that all may know Thy glory through the Holy Spirit.

O Lord, grant to all nations to know Thee by Thy Holy Spirit. As Thou didst give the Holy Spirit to the apostles and they knew Thee, so grant to all people to know Thee by Thy Holy Spirit.

O brethren, I beg and pray you in the name of God's compassion, believe in the Gospels and in the witness of the Holy Church and you will, while still here on earth, savour the blessedness of paradise, for the Kingdom of God is within us: with the love of God the soul knows paradise.

Who is there that can realize what paradise is? He who bears with him in the Holy Spirit can realize it in part, since paradise is the Kingdom of the Holy Spirit, and the Holy Spirit both in heaven and on earth is One and the Same. [Wisdom from Mount Athos]

RESOURCES

Editor's note: The following list of resources has been divided into three categories—modern authors, liturgical services and writings of Eastern Orthodox Saints. Most of the works which fall into the former two categories are in print and easily available. Many of the books containing the writings of the Saints are now out of print. The titles cited below should, however, be available in large public libraries or those of theological seminaries.

MODERN AUTHORS

BULGAKOV, SERGIUS, *The Orthodox Church*, Trans. Elizabeth S. Cram; ed. Donald A. Lowrie, London: The Centenary Press 1935, New York: Morehouse, 1935.

CABASILAS, NICHOLAS, *The Life in Christ*, Crestwood, New York: St. Vladimir's Press, 1974.

FEDOTOV, GEORGE, *A Treasury of Russian Spirituality*, New York: Sheed and Ward, 1948.

FLOROVSKY, GEORGES, *Bible, Church, Tradition. An Eastern Orthodox View*, Belmont, Mass.: Nordland Press, 1972.

LOSSKY, VLADIMIR, *The Mystical Theology of the Eastern Church*, London: J. Clarke, 1957.

LOSSKY, VLADIMIR, *In the Image and Likeness of God*, Crestwood, New York: St. Vladimir's Press, 1974.

MEYENDORF, JOHN, *St. Gregory Palamas and Orthodox Spirituality*, Crestwood, New York: St. Vladimir's Press, 1974.

SCHMEMANN, ALEXANDER, *For the Life of the World, Sacraments and Orthodoxy*, Crestwood, New York: St. Vladimir's Press, 1973.

SCHMEMANN, ALEXANDER, *Of Water and the Spirit*, Crestwood, New York: St. Vladimir's Press, 1975.

SCHMEMANN, ALEXANDER, ed. *Ultimate Questions. An Anthology of Modern Russian Religious Thought*, essay, "On the Holy Spirit" by Fr. Pavel Florensky, New York: Holt, Rinehart, & Winston, 1965.

ZANDER, VALENTINE, *Saint Seraphim of Sarov*, Crestwood, New York: St. Vladimir's Press, 1975.

LITURGICAL SERVICES

The Divine Liturgy, Orthodox Church in America, 1967, New York.

The Festal Menaion, Texts of the Major Feasts of the Eastern Orthodox Church, Trans. Mother Mary and Archimandrite Kallistos Ware, London, 1969.

Service Book of the Holy Orthodox-Catholic Apostolic Church, Tr. I.F. Hopgood, New York, 1956.

SAINTS

ATHANASIUS THE GREAT, "Letters to Serapion on the Holy Spirit," trans. and ed. C.R.B. Shapland, *The Letters of Saint Athanasius Concerning the Holy Spirit*, New York: Philosophical Library, 1951.

BASIL THE GREAT, "On the Holy Spirit" *A Select Library of Nicene and Post-Nicene Fathers of the Christian Church*, Trans. Blomfield Jackson, Second Series, Volume 8, New York: The Christian Literature Company, 1895.

GREGORY NAZIANZEN (The Theologian), "On the Holy Spirit, the Fifth Theological Oration" *A Select Library of Nicene and Post-Nicene Fathers of the Christian Church*, eds. Henry Wace and Philip Schaff, Second Series, Volume 7, New York: The Christian Literature Company, 1894.

GREGORY OF NYSSA, *From Glory to Glory, Selected Texts from Gregory of Nyssa's Mystical Writings*, Intro. by Jean Danielou, trans. and ed. Herbert Musurillo, New York: Scribner, 1961.

GREGORY OF NYSSA, *"On the Beatitudes and On the Lord's Prayer"* Ancient Christian Writers, Trans. Hilda C. Graet, Volume 18, Westminster, Md.: Newman Press, 1954.

JOHN CHRYSOSTOM "Homilies of St. John, St. Matthew and the Letters of St. Paul" *A Select Library of Nicene and Post-Nicene Fathers of the Christian Church*, ed. Philip Schaff, First Series, Volumes 10-14, New York: Christian Literature Co., 1888-90.

JOHN CLIMACUS, *The Ladder of Divine Ascent*, Intro. M. Heppell, Trans. Archimandrite Lazarus Moore, London: Faber and Faber, Ltd., 1959.

MACARIUS THE GREAT OF EGYPT, *Fifty Spiritual Homilies*, Willis, California: Eastern Orthodox Books, 1974.

MAXIMUS THE CONFESSOR, "The Ascetic Life" and "The Four Centuries on Chants" *Ancient Christian Writers*, trans. and ed. Polycarp Sherwood, Volume 21, Westminster, Md.: Newman Press, 1955.

SIMEON THE NEW THEOLOGIAN, *Hymns of Divine Love*, Trans. G. Maloney, Denville, N.J.: Dimension Books, 1975.

SILOUAN OF MOUNT ATHOS, *Wisdom from Mount Athos*, Intro. Archimandrite Sophrony, Crestwood, N.Y: St. Vladimir's Press, 1974.

Early Fathers from the Philokalia, Trans. Kedloubovsky and G.E.H. Palmer, London: Faber & Faber, Ltd., 1954.

Writings from the Philokalia on Prayer of the Heart, Trans. Kedloubovsky and G.E.H. Palmer, London: Faber & Faber, Ltd., 1951.